Community Connections: Intergenerational Links in Art Education

Angela M. La Porte, Editor

2004

NATIONAL ART EDUCATION ASSOCIATION

DEDICATION

This book is dedicated to my family and extended family.

About the National Art Education Association

The National Art Education Association is the world's largest professional art education association and a leader in educational research, policy, and practice for art education. NAEA's mission is to advance art education through professional development, service, advancement of knowledge, and leadership.

Membership (approximately 48,000) includes elementary and secondary art teachers (and middle and senior high students in the National Art Honor Society programs), artists, administrators, museum educators, arts council staff, and university professors from throughout the United States and several foreign countries. It also includes publishers, manufacturers and suppliers of art materials, parents, students, retired art educators, and others concerned about quality art education in our schools.

The Association publishes several journals, papers, and flyers on art education; holds an annual convention; conducts research; sponsors a teacher awards program; develops standards on student learning, school programs and teacher preparation; and cosponsors workshops, seminars and institutes on art education. For further information, contact our web site at www.naea-reston.org.

© 2004 National Art Education Association
1916 Association Drive
Reston, VA 20191

Order No. 202
ISBN 1-890160-26-1

Contents

INTRODUCTION

Intergenerational programs have become widespread since the mid-20th century, emphasizing "activities that increase cooperation and exchange between any two generations. Typically, they involve interaction between young and old in which there is a sharing of skills, knowledge, and experience" (Newman, 1986, p. 6). They developed in response to concerns that different age groups had become socially isolated from one another. Sociologists and gerontologists became convinced of the social and psychological benefits of intergenerational activities, such as elevated self-esteem and sense of autonomy among seniors and improved attitudes of each age cohort towards the other.

By the 1970s, the first intergenerational *art* programs were documented. They exploited these relationships further for educational purposes, to facilitate the exchange of historical and cultural understandings in art learning environments. These art programs are now commonplace, and while diverse in their approaches, they share a focus on rejuvenating social interactions between generations, which have languished since the early 20th century (e.g., Diamond, 1988; Erickson, 1983; La Porte, 2002; Newman, 1986; Perlstein & Bliss, 1994; Rogers, 1995). This book attempts to provide some tools and research directions with which to confront the insidious but pervasive effects of age segregation.

Separation by age, much like racial segregation, resulted from economic and demographic forces which brought unforeseen injury both to individuals and to their social relations with each other. Three generation households, a mainstay of the earlier agrarian economy, went into steep decline. Grandparents began to live apart from their children's families, hence the explosion of retirement villages, nursing homes, and public housing for the aged. The educational system segregates students into grade level by age, reducing interactions with those outside of their age group. And young people have their own cultural milieu loaded with values and imagery, seemingly a world apart from their elders. This physical and social separation often results in a proliferation of negative stereotypes, mistrust, even fear of those outside one's age group. Ideally, all citizens should feel themselves a valued part of their community, interacting, sharing, participating, contributing, learning from one another. That is how I remember my own youth.

Among my earliest, fondest memories are moments I shared with older relatives through the arts. I faintly recall sitting on my Uncle Carmen's lap at the age of 3 as he played the harmonica and taught me to sing "Oh, Susannah." He loved to share his music with me; "Who will sing to Angela?" he lamented, before he died. My 80-year-old grandmother also sang Italian folk songs while holding me in her arms. My sister and her friends introduced me to the world of the visual and performing arts at an impressionable age. She was 11 years older, a visual art major, and they were artists, musicians, actors, and writers. All inspired and encouraged me to compose poetry, play music and sing, act, and draw. My sister urged me to audition for a production of "The King and I" at the renowned Heinz Hall in Pittsburgh. Shy and inexperienced, I was astonished when I was selected to play the part of a princess and became an important part of a cast with older professional performerrs.

I remember the many hours I spent with Josephine, a neighbor in her 60s, making art while we discussed everything from fishing strategies to her cultural roots to what were profound philosophical questions for a 10-year-old. As a teenager, I was active in a community arts organization founded by my sister and her friends. The group encouraged people of all ages to participate in various artistic activities from drama to visual art. I felt right at home with this extended intergenerational family, bustling with engaging teenagers, adults, and older adults. And my longtime participation in community and church choirs has always afforded me spiritual and artistic sustenance as voices of all ages blend in a community of song. As I grow older, I look back on these nurturing experiences with deep gratitude and a firm conviction that my intergenerational art adventures expanded my world and enriched my mind and my life.

This book is intended to inform and energize an intergenerational movement in art education. Part I, composed of six chapters, includes some current research in the field of art education. Part II describes a variety of intergenerational programs across the United States. These contributions provide a foundation of research and curriculum from which stimulating new programs can evolve. They programs enrich and deepen the educational experience of the participants and promote many social and psychological benefits.

References

Diamond, D. (1988). The Pittsburgh story: Filling the grandparent gap. *50 Plus*, *28*(50), 42-51.

Ediger, M. (2002). *Evaluation of the community school concept*. (ERIC Document Reproduction Service No. ED461675)

Erickson, M. (1983). Teaching art history as an inquiry process. *Art Education*, *36*(5), 28-31.

La Porte, A. M. (2002). Intergenerational art education: Building community in Harlem. *The Journal of Social Theory in Art Education*, *22*(1), 51-71.

Newman, S. (1986). Sharing skills, experience key to interaction between young and old. *Perspective on Aging*, *15*(6), 6-7, 9.

Perlstein, S., & Bliss, J. (1994). *Generating community: Intergenerational partnerships through the expressive arts*. New York: Elders Share the Arts.

Rogers, A. M. (1995). *Intergenerational mentoring: Benefits and barriers for elder mentors*. (Dissertation, Temple University, 1994).

Preface

We can talk together, we can draw together, we can sing together, and we can think and exchange ideas together as equals, but we must approach each other as people, not as ages and stages. Yet, we cannot discount that the age cohorts we experience as we grow have very strong, long-lasting, and valid meanings in our lives.

Years before I became aware of the validity of intergenerational opportunities, I ran an early morning art session in my small school for a group of youngsters whose parents requested such a program. They ranged from kindergarten through 6th-grade. It was an incredible opportunity for me to see how they interrelated, and for them to exchange ideas beyond their usual age cohorts. Two 8th-graders were my assistants, and it was a grand learning experience all around. One unforgettable moment was the desire for Joey, a 5-year-old, to draw a person. He followed me around, with his paper and crayon, commenting, "I want to draw a person but I can't." After about five minutes of this, as I worked with others, I turned to him and said, "how can I help you if I can't see what you can do?" He looked at me, puzzled. Then he went to the table, and drew a wonderful person any 5-year-old would be proud of. "Well," I said, "you really can draw a person, and you did!" He beamed as others in the group nodded and commented about his work. By seeing what we can each do in the arts, by hearing others sing or dance, play an instrument, sculpt or paint, we realize that the arts belong to no age group, and that the same material can be manipulated and changed, whether in sound or shape or size, by whoever dares to try!

Growth and development in the visual arts need to be nurtured from birth through old age with authentic opportunities to function creatively. For many, regardless of age, the excitement and stimulation from art never ceases. When asked was he still painting in his 80s, Raphael Soyer replied, "Are you still breathing?" An 8-year-old said, "Art is something beautiful." An 85-year-old commented that "painting has become my spiritual life, NOT my hobby. I have a need to create, to put order in my ideas. It's like being in touch with God." An 11-year-old noted "art is working with your hands as well as your mind." A 94-year-old (in a nursing home) said, "I like painting so much I even dream about it." An 8-year-old said, "Art expresses what you think about things, what they tell you and what they look like to you." And finally, one youngster replied, "Art is something I have a temptation to do."

Intergenerational links can be made womb to tomb. Within a senior center, there are intergenerational possibilities as folks who are 65 mix with those who are 80. In a school setting, 6th-graders mixing with 3rd-graders and 2nd graders mixing with those in nursery school are creating intergenerational links. Considering that we are systematically age segregated all through school, often until the college level, we have a huge task learning how to work with mixed ages. Yet, we know that these links need to be made among the old and the young, the well and the ill, among those with experience in the arts, and those just daring to dip a toe into the world of the many different arts. The task offers challenges and joys, but most of all it offers us opportunities to learn from each other as we share ideas and experiences in an open flexible manner, understanding the fear some have and the pleasures we are preparing them (and ourselves) to experience.

Our editor has gathered wonderful chapters about intergenerational involvement with professional artists, children, teenagers, adults, older adults, performers, sculptors, photographers, musicians, quilters, museum programs and artifacts, artist books, documentary film works, and paintings large and small in a wide range of settings. This accumulated material, bolstered by our own good experiences, will help set us well on our way to grasping the many and varied approaches to intergenerational links in art education, and the realization that quality programs call for qualified faculty as teachers in any setting where the arts are taught!

Pearl Greenberg

Part I

The six chapters in Part I include current research in intergenerational art education. The editor begins with a general review of literature in the field of intergenerational art education including the educational, social, and psychological implications. Keys, Ferrell, and Passey follow with a case study involving at-risk youth, professional artists, the Boise Art Museum, and the local community in a program that encourages participants to share their lives by combining photography, text, and other media. Lawton examines the nature of the learning and social relationships that evolved during a book art program involving small groups of participants ages 14 to 82 at an inner-city senior day center. Tapley's intergenerational art class with university students and six senior citizens with life-long cognitive disabilities offers some documented evidence that intergenerational interaction positively influences their mental recall and their art. Zelkowitz presents a social action research project focusing on how a mural project with residents in a nursing home affects the personal development of high school students. The final chapter focuses on art teachers' experiences learning about Southwest Native American pottery led by a Tribal Clan Grandmother through immersing themselves into the culture of the Acoma people. Since research in intergenerational art education is sparse, the contributions made by these authors are welcomed with hopes of identifying best practices for bringing people of different ages together through the arts and creating a foundation on which we can build the success of future programs.

1

Angela M. La Porte

The Educational, Social, And Psychological Implications Of Intergenerational Art Education

Intergenerational Programs

Intergenerational programs emerged in the United States during the 1960s and encompassed many "activities that increase cooperation and exchange between any two generations. Typically, they involve interaction between the young and the old in which there is a sharing of skills, knowledge and experience" (Newman, 1986, p. 6). Participants may vary in age from preschool to adults over 90 and may come from any socioeconomic level and cultural background. Some older persons may have physical or mental limitations or special needs. Programs may meet in public schools, museums, senior centers, nursing homes or various other sites in the community. Near the middle of the 20th century, gerontologists, psychologists, educators, and specialists in human development began to realize that the structure and demographics of our society were dramatically changing, and they became concerned that this change was having negative consequences. Three crucial factors were: (a) the relative increase in the older adult population, (b) the growing number of age-segregated communities, and (c) the decreasing interaction between younger and older family members. Documented effects of the changes included loneliness and a decline in self-esteem among older adults, a decrease in children's awareness of their cultural and historical background, a fear of aging in the young, and an increase in negative stereotypes of each age group for the other.

Generally, the research literature on intergenerational programming measures social or psychological benefits for participants, such as children's attitudinal perceptions toward older adults, older adults' impressions of children, and how contact with youth improved the life satisfaction for older adults. Metcalf (1990) and Rogers (1995) considered seniors' attitudes toward intergenerational volunteerism and mentoring, noting these activities positively affected older adults' perceptions of young people. Feniak (1993) and Patten (1994) found that the negative attitudes that both age groups had about the other diminished following intergenerational interactions.

Newman, Vasuder, and Baum (1983) studied the life satisfaction of 350 senior center volunteers at three different intergenerational program sites using a variety of methods, including questionnaires, standardized life satisfaction index, semi-structured interviews and personal data forms. All participants acknowledged personal gratification, and improvements in self-esteem and life satisfaction. Many volunteers who suffered the death or illness of a loved one noted an alleviation of negative emotions.

A longitudinal study by Newman, Karip, and Faux (1994) with 26 intergenerational program volunteers age 60 and older concluded that well educated volunteers improved memory function by 8.9 percent, and less educated volunteers experienced a memory increase of 2.1 percent at the conclusion of the 8-month program, based on the Rivermead Behavioral Memory Test and on a memory function questionnaire.

Diamond (1988) cited a variety of benefits from an older adult artist-in-residence school volunteer program. He reported that over 350 older participants "found life more satisfying" (p. 48). Intergenerational involvement with children at local schools helped seniors cope with traumatic life experiences. Elders also increased their sense of self-esteem and autonomy in their community. According to Newman, et al., (1985), such structured activities as volunteering in schools improved life satisfaction, self-worth, and overall mental health. Children who received assistance during school tended to improve their grades and behavior. Attitude toward aging improved among those who rarely saw their grandparents and previously had held a negative view of aging.

Most intergenerational research has taken place in the fields of gerontology and sociology, typically, documenting attempts to reduce cultural and age-related stereotypes, prevent depression, and improve self-worth among older adults. Few studies have investigated the quality of learning or sharing between the old and young during visual art programs. Older adults have served as resources for understanding art objects, as artists who taught their skills to students, or as equal partners in a reciprocal interaction. The emphasis of many intergenerational programs has revolved around reminiscence of the elder's remote past, often, an undiminished asset. However, little formal study of visual art programs and their efficacy has been documented. Few researchers have considered the educational potential and contextual learning implications for art education.

Historical Overview of Intergenerational Programs

Newman (1980), noted that many intergenerational programs had been con-ducted or were currently being developed. At senior citizen centers, children and adolescents have participated in oral history projects, and in art, music, fitness, and other activities with elders. Older persons have served as role models and support persons to young residents of social institutions, prisons, hospitals, and agencies for child services. They have volunteered as tutors, career models, hobbyists, and friends in schools, and have contributed to the social, emotional, and academic development of children. School-aged children have visited nursing homes, exchanged physical and psychological support for knowledge, and established friendships in many ways. Some older adult volunteers have worked with mentally retarded children in creative dance, drama, music, and muscle development. Older adults have shared knowledge with university students. Retirees have participated in advising at their former place of employ-ment. Community centers and YMCAs have long offered activities for all ages. Regardless of the differences in purpose and activity, intergenerational programs share a common goal of nurturing the natural relationships between diverse age groups that have always been at the heart of a healthy community.

The earliest application of the intergenerational concept, bringing generations together, originated with John Dewey's community school project in Missouri during the 1910s and 1920s. The public school building became the center for neighborhood activities, encouraging an open exchange of communication and socialization between all members of the community, regardless of age. Dewey believed that learning experiences between various ages were important for a more democratic society in order to compensate for an increasingly common phenomenon of the time, age separation (Dewey, 1916; Ediger, 2002). Ruggles (2003) attributed this development to the transition from a society of agrarian and occupational inheritance to one of wage labor.

Forty years later, many intergenerational programs emerged in the United States, encouraging conversational exchange between generations and providing tutorial services for children. Some of the more distinguished ones are described here. The first documented intergenerational program began in New York City in 1963 as the *Foster Grandparents Program*. The Office of Economic Opportunity established it as a Community Action Project to "demonstrate the capabilities of lower income older persons" (Newman, 1989, p. 2) in supportive grandparent roles nurturing the development of children. It joined the Volunteer ACTION network in 1965, matching healthy older adults with special needs children (Newman, 1989). The P. K. Yonge Laboratory School at the University of Florida developed the *Adopt a Grandparent Program* in 1963 (Whitley, et al., 1976). Classes of young children visited nearby convalescent homes on a weekly basis to converse with residents.

The Community Service Society of Staten Island, New York, established *Serve and Enrich Retirement by Volunteer Experience* (*SERVE*) from 1967-69. Funded by federal and local grants and the Community Service Society, the program enlisted retired persons to provide community service. The project began with 23 older adult volunteers who worked with mentally retarded children and young adults at a residential home. *SERVE* grew to involve 1,500 senior volunteers and was the catalyst for the Retired Senior Volunteer Program (*RSVP*) in New York City. *SERVE* later merged with *RSVP*, serving five boroughs within the city. By 1971 there were 750 *RSVP* programs across the country with 400,000 older adult volunteers (Sainer & Zander, 1971).

A novel program began in 1978 at Messiah Village in Mechanicsburg, Pennsylvania, involving daily scheduled interaction between the children of a childcare center and a nearby dependent-care retirement center (Newman, 1989). Today, these types of connections exist at numerous sites across the nation. In many cases, these facilities are built in locations that make intergenerational interactions more accessible and convenient.

Research on many of these early programs contributed to an expansive body of literature on the topic in the fields of sociology and gerontology. Over 1,000 pages of article, book, document, and video citations can be found at http://intergenerational.cas.psu.edu/IGResourceList.html, a web site created by Abigail Lawrence at the University of Michigan. It is available through a database set up by Matt Kaplan, an Intergenerational Programs and Aging Specialist at the Pennsylvania State University. Unfortunately, this extensive catalog refers to only two pages of visual and performing arts references.

The Intergenerational Community School has recently taken the intergenerational concept into a public charter school in Cleveland, Ohio. The founders promote a "multipolar" and "multidirectional" approach to education including interactions between various age groups at the school and with people in the community. "Multipolar" refers to a focus on the interaction between all ages, broadening the traditional connections between the old and young. The school is "multidirectional" in that it addresses the educational needs of everyone in the community. The philosophy offers educational, social, and psychological benefits to everyone, not targeting any two distinct age groups. "Such multiage communities of learners represent a conceptual and organizational response to the challenges that rapid cultural and environmental change and resultant alienation are posing for human societies" (Whitehouse, et al., 2000, p. 761).

Intergenerational Art Programs

The number of documented intergenerational *art* programs is limited compared to those in sociology and gerontology. One of the earliest recorded attempts to integrate art into an intergenerational setting, developed in the 1970s, involved using studio instruction in arts and crafts. Streitfeld (1976) described a 5-month program she conducted at the Hebrew Home for the Aged in New York City in 1973, introducing six troubled adolescents to an arts and crafts program. Despite some difficulties during an initial period of adjustment, Streitfeld noted substantial gains in self-esteem among the elders as a result of their feeling needed and receiving genuine praise from the youngsters for their art.

Many programs give elders the opportunity to teach their skills to younger students. The Pioneer Settlement for the Creative Arts, Inc., founded in 1976 by art teachers in Florida, educates students about traditional folk art, blacksmithing, woodworking and pottery. In 1978, *Generations Together*, a similar intergenerational exchange program affiliated with the University of Pittsburgh, developed intergenerational program models, researched them, and disseminated information on program development as part of The Intergenerational Arts and Education Program (IAEP). Older adult artists, age 50 and up, visit classrooms throughout the Pittsburgh area and teach children about their artmaking techniques. The Goldman Institute on Aging in San Francisco also places seniors in teaching roles that are cross-generational and cross-cultural.

Elders Share the Arts (*ESTA*), a prominent community arts organization in Brooklyn, New York, originated in 1979. Their staff of professional educators, social workers, and artists bring seniors and young people together, transforming personal oral histories into visual artworks, drama, and literature. *ESTA* employs an oral history format, integrating the history and culture of individuals into an arts medium through intergenerational exchange. Their program objective has been to break through the generational and cultural divisions among residents in diverse New York City neighborhoods in order to nurture a shared sense of community among them (Perlstein & Bliss, 1994).

The Learning Guild, Incorporated, of Boston, Massachusetts published a handbook for Intergenerational Humanities Programs (IHP) in 1980. An IHP creates "long-term relationships between the generations based on their common interests in the humanities" (p. 4). The handbook includes an overview of the program, suggestions for pairing community organizations, and for planning and implementation.

During the 1980s, art educators began to acknowledge the educational implications of intergenerational art situations. Erickson (1983) noted that art historical inquiry could be enhanced by arranging for students to interview older acquaintances or relatives about a period of time and a place while studying relevant artworks or artifacts. Kauppinen (1988) suggested that older adults are assets for discussing and understanding art, often identifying motifs, symbols and literary themes by their familiarity with Biblical stories, events from history, and myths.

Stokrocki (1988) asserted that "crossing age boundaries can create unique bonds—and unique art" (p. 40). She described an environmental mural project involving the assistance of a professional muralist, junior high school students, and senior citizens from the nearby community. Stokrocki noted that the intergenerational interaction and sharing of art skills "were the most valuable aspects of the program" (p. 40).

One of the earliest published books including intergenerational art lessons was by Davis and Ferdman in 1993. Their themes focused on personal histories, family traditions, folk arts, local histories, family folklore, and national history, encouraging older members of the community to contribute their rich knowledge of art, artistic tradition, culture, and experience to the art classroom (Guay, 1995).

A "singing quilt" project implemented by Diane Barret (1996) helped community members develop a better understanding of the history and aesthetics of African-American quilting in a 3-county area near Athens, Georgia. Senior citizens from the area shared their quilting craft through demonstrations of technique, personal histories, and traditional hymns. Each senior citizen and high school student contributed one square toward a community quilt that was displayed at the culmination of the program. The seniors' squares illustrated hymns while the selected student themes symbolized a song that was important to them. The teenagers' interaction with seniors brought the aesthetics of African-American quiltmaking to life. Each group learned together about the other during historical lectures on quilting, storytelling, and singing, and from making a 24-square quilt together.

Zuk and Dalton (2000) described School Connects with Community, a community-based program in Igloonik, Canada. Young people interviewed parents and older adults in their community and collected stories and artifacts related to the community's culture. Elders depicted their life experiences and culture for the younger generation through drawings of hunting stories, seals, and other representations of the community's traditions and history, illustrating their cultural heritage and the changes that have affected their community.

The Steel Industry Heritage Corporation of Homestead, Pennsylvania developed curricula and organized partnerships between schools and older folk and traditional artists in southwestern Pennsylvania. The organization trained quilters, wood carvers, embroiderers and others to bring the ethnic and historical aesthetic of their art to children while promoting multicultural understanding and cultural acceptance within the community (Deafenbaugh, 1997).

Another program in Pennsylvania brought together high school students and older adults from Philadelphia through a Teaching Tolerance grant. It developed a theatrical workshop, an oral history publication based on interviews, and a mural painting reflecting the backgrounds of the participants (Bolling, 2004). In Miami-Dade County, high school student journalists annually collect biographies from seniors in the community to learn about history, social, and cultural studies based on a new theme every year. Students also draw portraits of the interviewees to be printed in a booklet with their biographies to preserve the community's history.

An ethnographic study of an intergenerational art program in New York City's Harlem involving Hispanic and African American teenagers and homebound older adults is one of the few research studies conducted by an art educator (La Porte, 2002). Social and educational implications for art education emerged during the 7-month intergenerational relationships. Social service, oral history, and art making provided a natural setting for the emergence of community (i.e., a group of people who have mutual respect and understanding for one another and participate freely in dialogue regardless of ethnicity, age, and/or gender). Students collected oral histories of volunteer senior citizens during interviews and discussion about culturally and historically relevant artwork. All participants collaborated in the creation of collages based on the oral histories. The exchange of personal history and culture generated understanding and respect, and reduced age-related stereotypes. The intergenerational interactions empowered both age groups and engendered a sense of community between young people and senior citizens from local housing projects. Oral history discussions pro-

8

vided an interesting and contextual approach to learning about artworks through inquiry and the sharing of life experiences. Intergenerational exchanges during art making added a relaxed, unintimidating setting; art training became more focused and meaningful when older adults were present.

Over the past few years, the National Art Education Association and the International Society for Education through Art conferences have included numerous presentations on intergenerational topics. Some of those presenters are contributing authors in this book. A growing number of intergenerational art programs exist that have not been studied or documented. Additional scholarly research will help define some desirable objectives and best practices; some preliminary suggestions follow.

Recommendations and Accommodations for Intergenerational Programs

The development of intergenerational programs should begin with an understanding between the organizations and persons involved to establish common goals and objectives as well as an outline of procedures and activities, and a timeline for their realization (Newman, 1986). Regular cooperation and timely communication are essential throughout the process.

A clarification of the objectives, guidelines, and responsibilities of all persons involved should be provided through orientation and training. According to Newman (1986), all participants must have a clear understanding of goals and objectives and of their roles and responsibilities.

Funding sources must be adequate to cover all related expenses. This will help to avoid difficulties that may interfere with program planning and quality. For example, in the Harlem art program, social services became an integral component that secured funding provided by the city, but art-related activities languished, unfunded for many weeks. This shift to a social service emphasis early in the program did have an unexpected benefit. Social services became a vehicle for establishing familiarity between participants that later helped create a more relaxed and open dialogue between the teenagers and older adults. While seniors who rarely interact with young people may develop dislike, fear, and mistrust towards them, social service visits and casual conversations helped reduce the problem. Discussions about childhood experiences also offered a common ground, allowing the elders to empathize with the young and allow the young to see their seniors in a new light as people who had once been their age, which appeared to reduce anxiety among both age groups.

Most important, facilitators should involve participants in program design whenever this is feasible. Seniors may be sensitive to certain topics, and it is important to solicit themes, questions, and ideas in which they have an interest. Participants become more immediately engaged and alert when dialogue revolves around such topics. Beginning with familiar dialogue and moving beyond it can engage students in discussing issues they previously didn't consider relevant to their lives.

Difficulties related to intergenerational programs may derive from mental, physical, cultural, and/or gender-oriented incompatibilities between the two populations. Young students often prefer fast-paced interaction modes, whereas older adults would rather work at a slower pace, both mentally and physically, or may be hampered by mental or physical ailments. Languages, customs, and beliefs may vary among residents of the same community. The latter differences may be a concern for teachers or coordinators in designing the most beneficial and appropriate matching of children with adults. In addition, attention to subtleties of gender roles and interactions across culture and class can help navigate obstacles to the fluid exchange of historical and cultural knowledge.

Many older adults exhibit common mental and physical deficiencies related to long-term memory abilities (Kauppinen, 1990; Wald, 1983) and divergent thinking (Jacobowitz & Shanan, 1982). Short-term memory may be affected but usually not recall of the distant past, except in the event of certain cognitive disabilities. These reminiscences can be a valuable asset for uncovering histori- cal information about one's community and should be considered during program planning. Seniors love to talk once they feel comfortable, but may tend to wander off on tangents. Unrelated topics can easily be refocused toward program goals with thoughtful question planning and strategy.

Physical deficiencies related to hearing (Kingston, 1982; Hoffman, 1992), speed (Jacobowitz & Shanan, 1982) and dexterity (Hoffman, 1992) should be identi- fied and accommodations made. Speak in a clear, full voice for the benefit of the hard of hearing, and encourage others to do the same. Be aware that subtle or even well-defined color variations may not be distinct to the vision impaired (Stanford & Pollack, 1984). Older adults may require more time to work and respond to questions. Less complex art activities may be necessary when dexterity is an issue.

Finally, research should include the collection of ongoing and final evaluations from participants. These are valuable for planning future intergenerational programs. It is also advisable to meet regularly with the people and organiza- tions involved to reaffirm goals, guidelines, and responsibilities, and to work out difficulties. Although other issues might arise due to the environmental and participant contexts, general guidelines are applicable in most situations. Well designed intergenerational interactions will offer the greatest possibility for educational, social, and psychological benefits, avoiding a variety of difficult and frustrating situations.

Conclusion

Intergenerational art programs are well established and growing across the United States. Yet, there is a need for more intergenerational art education research in the 21st century that considers how to restructure our education in art to meet the needs of the current growth in our population's diversity, including separations that exist between age, culture, and socioeconomic groups.

Art educators need to embrace and elaborate upon Dewey's community school concept to a broader, more inclusive community where interaction is encouraged between all people, regardless of age, socioeconomic level, ethnicity, gender, etc. But to date, they have done little formal investigation into the advantages and difficulties of interactive relationships between generations, even less consideration of age differences in conjunction with diversity in the culture, social class, and gender of participants. There is ample evidence that intergenerational relationships benefit both young and old socially and psycho-logically. I also believe that, given the growing diversity of our neighborhoods, sharing knowledge across generations can help build a continuum of history and culture, providing a shared sense of community, making a substantial contribu-tion to a healthier society.

References

Alexenberg, M. (2000). *Intergenerational collaboration in public art*. Los Angeles: Paper presented at the conference of the National Art Education Association.

Barret, D. B. (1996). *Singing quilts: Rhythm, improvisation, and narrative in two African-American creative forms*. Athens, GA: Final report to the Georgia Council for the Arts, Folklife Program.

Bolling, A. (2004). Eldergrace: Pennsylvania programs promote respect across generations. *Teaching Tolerance, 25*(1), 14-15.

Davis, S., & Ferdman, B. (1993). *Nourishing the heart*. New York: City Lore, Inc. and Creative Ways.

Deafenbaugh, L. (1997). *Community-based folk arts in the classroom*. New Orleans: Paper presented at the conference of the National Art Education Association.

Dewey, J. (1916). *Democracy and education*. New York: The Macmillan Company.

Diamond, D. (1988). The Pittsburgh story: Filling the grandparent gap. *50 Plus, 28*(50), 42-51.

Ediger, M. (2002). *Evaluation of the community school concept.* (ERIC Document Reproduction Service No. ED461675)

Erickson, M. (1983). Teaching art history as an inquiry process. *Art Education, 36*(5), 28-31.

Feniak, M. A. (1993). *Effects of an intergenerational program on children's and teachers' attitudes towards aging and seniors' attitudes towards volunteering in the schools.* (Master's Thesis, University of Windsor).

Guay, D. M. (1995). The sunny side of the street: A supportive community for the inclusive art classroom. *Art Education, 48*(3), 51-56.

Intergenerational humanities program handbook. (1980). Boston, MA: The Learning Guild.

Hoffman, D. H. (1992). *Arts for older adults: An enhancement of life.* Englewood Cliffs, NJ: Prentice Hall.

Jacobowitz, J., & Shanan, J. (1982). Higher education for the second half of life. The state of the art and future perspectives. *Educational Gerontology, 6,* 545-564.

Kauppinen, H. (1988). Discussing art with older adults. *Art Education, 41*(6), 14-19.

Kauppinen, H. (1990). Changing perspectives on older adults' mental abilities and educational needs: Implications for art education. *Studies in Art Education, 31*(2), 99-105.

Kingston, A. J. (1982). Attitudes and problems of elderly students in the university system of Georgia. *Educational Gerontology, 8*(1), 87-92.

La Porte, A. M. (2002). Intergenerational art education: Building community in Harlem. *The Journal of Social Theory in Art Education, 22*(1), 51-71.

Metcalf, B. G. (1990). *Attitudes of older persons about volunteering and willingness to participate in an intergenerational education program* (generation networking). (Dissertation, Loma Linda University, 1990.)

Newman, S. (1980). *Rationale for linking the generations together.* National Council on Aging Mini-Conference. University of Georgia: Athens, GA.

Newman, S. (1986). Sharing skills, experience key to interaction between young and old. *Perspective on Aging, 15*(6), 6-7, 9.

Newman, S. (1989). A history of intergenerational programs. In S. Newman & S. W. Brummel (Eds.), *Intergenerational programs: Imperatives, strategies, impacts, trends.* New York: The Haworth Press.

Newman, S., Karip, E., & Faux, R. B. (1994). *Everyday memory function of older adults, the impact of intergenerational school volunteer programs.* Unpublished paper.

Newman, S., Lyons, C., & Onawola, R. S. T. (1985). The development of an intergenerational service-learning program at a nursing home. *The Gerontologist, 25*(2), 130-133.

Newman, S., Vasuder, J., & Baum, M. (1983). *Final report to Andrus Foundation*, 1-90.

Newman, S., Vasuder, J., & Onawola, R. (1984). Older volunteers' perceptions of volunteering on their psychological well-being. *Journal of Applied Gerontology, 4*(2), 123-127.

Patten, M. H. (1994). *The effects of two types of intergenerational programs on preschool children's attitudes toward the elderly.* (Master's Thesis, Concordia University, Canada, 1993.)

Perlstein, S., & Bliss, J. (1994). *Generating community: Intergenerational partnerships through the expressive arts.* New York: Elders Share the Arts.

Rogers, A. M. (1995). *Intergenerational mentoring: Benefits and barriers for elder mentors.* (Dissertation, Temple University, 1994.)

Ruggles, L. (2003). Multigenerational families in nineteenth-century America. *Continuity and Change, 18*(1), 139-165.

Sainer, J. & Zander, M. (1971). *SERVE: Older volunteers in community service.* New York: Community Service Sociaty of New York.

Stanford, T. & Pollack, R. H. (1984). Configuration color vision tests: The interaction between aging and the complexity of figure-ground segregation. *Journal of Gerontology, 39,* 568-571.

Stokrocki, M. L. (1988). Art spans the generations. *School Arts, 88*(1), 40-41.

Streitfeld, E. (1976). Young and old together. *Social Policy, 7*(30), 100-102.

Wald, J. (1983). Alzheimer's disease and the role of art therapy in its treatment. *Art Therapy, 22,* 57-64.

Whitehouse, P. J., Bendezu, E., Fallcreek, S., & Whitehouse, C. (2000). Intergenerational community schools: A new practice for a new time. *Educational Gerontology, 26*(8), 761-770.

Whitley, E., Duncan, R., McKenzie, P., & Sledjeski, S. (1976). *From time to time: A record of young children's relationships with aged.* (Research Monograph No. 17). Gainesville, FL: University of Florida, PK. Yonge Laboratory School. (ERIC Document Reproduction Service No. ED128088.)

Zuk, B., & Dalton, R. (1996). Elders and art education. *InSEA News, 3*(3), 13-14.

Zuk, B., & Dalton, R. (2000). *Intergenerational and cross-age art experiences.* Los Angeles: Paper presented at the conference of the National Art Education Association.

2

*Kathleen Keys, Heather Ferrell,
and Karen Willie Passey*

Intergenerational Explorations Of *Snapshots: Lives In Transition*

Snapshots: Lives in Transition was a multidimensional art project involving at-risk youth[1], professional artists, the Boise Art Museum, and the community in Boise, Idaho. For three years this successful, Idaho Commission for the Arts funded project gave 30 to 40 at-risk youth the opportunity to use journaling and mixed-media art production to reflect upon their lives. Working with three to four professional artists, students created artworks using photographs, text, drawing, collage, and found objects. These artworks and artist statements were shown at a professional local gallery and at the Boise Art Museum. *Snapshots* not only enabled students to share their artistic talents and insights, but also encouraged multi-generational relationships between teenage students, local artists, professionals, and community members that will have a lasting impact on youth as well as adults.

Figure: 2.1 Genea Weaver, *What More Could a Girl Ask For?*, 2002, mixed media collage. "Don't try to help, just turn your head. I'll continue this cutting until I'm dead. Feel the pain inside my brain with each cut, feel the release, feel the calmness, feel the peace."

The art program developed out of conversations between Heather Ferrell, associate curator of art at Boise Art Museum, and Karen Willie Passey, Work and Learn[2] English teacher. These two coordinators collaborated in designing, directing, and implementing the project. They selected local professional artists based on their artistic merit as well as their perceived ability to work and to relate with youth. Invited artists included: Eve-Marie Bergren, Karen Bubb, Noble Hardesty, Surel Mitchell and Todd Newman. Passey and Ferrell created photography and journal assignments that helped the students to generate material for their own artworks.

Youth who participated in *Snapshots* were students at Work and Learn School. Although the primary goal of Work and Learn is to provide students who might otherwise be unable to attend school the opportunity to earn high school credit or a GED, the school also encourages artistic and creative expression and community involvement. Work and Learn School, the primary site for the *Snapshots* project, consists of four classrooms: two academic classrooms, an art room, and a computer room housed in a modular building. There is also a commons area and a conference room that are used as workspaces for the project.

Spanning 12 weeks in the spring, *Snapshots* is organized into weekly work sessions with each guest artist leading a different artmaking project. Students attended a museum photography exhibition, participated in lectures and activities focusing on contemporary photography, and photographed their lives with the aid of guided assignments and 35mm cameras. Concurrently, students responded to weekly journal prompts relating to the photography assignment and theme of each guest artist's project. Using their photographs and journals, students worked with local artists of varying ages to create mixed-media works of art. Every two weeks, a different artist led the project, and then returned several times to assist students in completing three or four final artworks. In culmination, students refined artworks and writings for final selection and exhibition. Every year, public venues were secured to exhibit *Snapshots* and included the private for profit Stewart Gallery, Boise Art Museum, and the Boise airport.

The first goals for *Snapshots* revolved around the students. The project gave at-risk students an opportunity to explore, to express, and to share their lives through photography, text, and other media. Students learned to better understand contemporary photography and art. More importantly, students worked directly with local artists and art professionals, and from this experience, developed positive intergenerational relationships with adults in their community. Other goals for the project focused on community impact. Artists developed professionally as they refined their teaching skills and explored their role as mentors, and the community developed a better understanding and appreciation of the lives, insights, and talents of the disenfranchised youth in their community. Backed by integral support from the Idaho Commission on the Arts, *Snapshots* created a new, collaborative partnership between Work and Learn School, Boise Art Museum, Stewart Gallery, as well as community businesses and individuals who also helped finance the project.

Since Work and Learn is a small alternative school, scheduling *Snapshots* into the school curriculum was relatively easy. The Work and Learn staff was flexible and willing to shorten academic and elective periods on Fridays to provide an hour and a half for the program or adjust their classes if more time was needed. Because *Snapshots* involved the entire school, the nine Work and Learn staff members, including academic teachers, the art teacher, the secretary, youth companions, and the social worker, were available to manage, supervise, and assist the students with their artwork.

Intergenerational Significance of *Snapshots: Lives in Transition*

Project coordinators partnered with a community-based art education researcher and worked to explore the intergenerational significance of *Snapshots* while highlighting the importance of collective, reflexive-practitioner research, and discussing community connections in art education. Limited prior analysis of *Snapshots* consisted of informal participant evaluations, community feedback, and basic grant evaluation reports to record the project's impacts and disseminate the results in informal ways. Later, qualitative data regarding the *Snapshots* project was compiled through a facilitated course of communal ethnographic interviews consisting of focus groups[3] of diverse intergenerational players (students, project coordinators/facilitators/school and museum staff, professional artists, and audience members) who through reflecting upon the project, identified the artistic, educational, social, and psychological implications of this innovative program.

Figure: 2.2 Christopher Leitch, *Doin' Time*, 2003, mixed-media shadow box

"*Doin' Time*. I named it this because it is about prison life and the time that is lost . . . being kept away from my family and not living the life that I wanted."

Artistic Implications

Regardless of their generational differences, *Snapshots* participants expanded their notions of the educational value and worth of art and artistic processes. For students, the artistic implications of the project encompassed major shifts in their definitions and perceptions of art and the process of making art. It is important to note that Idaho students' experience with art education is severely limited, with very few professional art instructors for elementary school, sporadic instruction in junior high, and consistent professional art instruction found only in high school where students *elect* to take art. In *Snapshots*, students became aware that art includes many disciplines beyond drawing with paper and pencil (i.e., painting/collage on saw blades or mufflers or working with encaustic). They also realized that mistakes and revision are an acceptable, inherent aspect of creating art. Combining art and writing, students communicated their personal lives using unfamiliar processes and initially daunting materials. Additionally, they responded to a rather intimidating invitation to become artists. Rather than working toward a dictated visual result (that may characterize previous experiences with creating art), students shared in an organic, collaborative endeavor with experimental and inexact conclusions.

Artists translated the essence of artistic practice (normally performed in isolation) to a public teaching realm. The new role of teacher was strange and intimidating for them. Artists experienced personal growth when challenged to communicate ideas to students in non-visual ways. These important communications included information regarding their own artistic concepts and processes. Todd Newman's project required students to collage photographs and text on paper and apply designs to car mufflers. Although Newman had successfully created his sample piece in the studio, he faced several challenges while leading the students in the project in terms of time, materials, and final presentation. When questioned about how his own artistic processes had been influenced by *Snapshots*, Newman observed, "I've just really refined it to where I can do a really decent piece for myself in three or four days. But again they only have a few hours . . . so they helped me think about my process" (Newman, artists focus group interview).

During Friday sessions the artist, Work and Learn staff, and project coordinators served as guides outlining the basic requirements and steps of the project, offering possibilities for creative problem-solving and encouraging participants. Non-arts Work and Learn staff witnessed first hand how complex concepts could be engaged and taught through art and writing, experiencing their integrative potential. Staff were especially intrigued by the visual components of the project and sought to participate alongside students as individual artists themselves.

Educational Implications

One misconception of the *Snapshots* project was that it educationally benefited only the Work and Learn students. Collectively, the different generations embodied by students, project coordinators, school staff, and artists discovered that learning (facilitated in this case by the creative art process) is an ongoing, lifelong practice that benefits all intergenerational players.

As in the real world, students learned that as artists they must work very hard to complete their artworks, and despite their efforts, their individual works may still not be selected for final exhibition. Completed works were subject to the selection processes of art curator, teacher, and artists. Because Work and Learn students constantly rotate in and out of the school, a final group project was presented at the end of each year's program. These artworks had firmer parameters and were installed in a group format. This allowed students who arrived at the end of the project and those who did not complete the other assignments to still be included in the exhibition. Nonetheless, students experienced the angst and tension related to creating artwork to be shared in school, juried, and potentially exhibited in the greater realm of the public at a professional gallery, museum, or civic space. Furthermore, students rejected the perception of art as *busy work*; instead, a new understanding of art making as an ongoing, evolving process that is both challenging and valuable became clear.

Paralleling the students' preliminary attitudes about being/becoming successful artists, project facilitators (other than the two main project coordinators) met the *Snapshots* project with initial skepticism and uncertainty about its possibility of success in the face of its complexity. One Work and Learn teacher explained her perception of *Snapshots'* desired final result, "I didn't get it until I saw it framed . . . I was there the whole time, and I've been to a museum before, but I really don't feel like I got it that first year" (Swanson, coordinators focus group interview). Moreover, these non-arts professionals experienced the rich potential of art for teaching and learning about the expression of complex issues such as identity, image, and personal history. Thus, *Snapshots,* with its synthesis of visual art and writing, illuminated the importance and possibilities for integrating art into more *academically* labeled studies. This year, Work and Learn's resident art teacher and a youth companion developed their own art project and are seeking arts council funding through their first grant application.

Artists found the project surprisingly educational, as they considered how to teach and refine their specific artistic process while verbalizing the themes in their work and their relation to *Snapshots*. Reciprocal learning occurred between artists and students enabling artists to consider and formulate ideas in their personal work. Most artists considered their involvement in the project as a rich, multi-layered professional development opportunity. Some artists had not considered teaching or application to the state arts council's artist-in-residence roster until after completing the project.

> I would have never worked with Melanie [curator of education] at the art museum—I would never have even considered [teaching a youth class] because I would have been so sure that I couldn't do it. So, for me [*Snapshots*] was really a step, giving me the idea of doing the artist roster. (Mitchell, artists focus group interview)

Artists also cited the extreme importance of discussing their work with others and gaining experience presenting themselves in public as artists. Encaustic artist, Eve-Marie Bergren explained,

> You go in there and you think—"oh my gosh what would a 14 to 18 year old be interested in hearing?" You are constantly revising and thinking about how you are going to present yourself. That aspect of presenting yourself to the public over and over again as an artist—you know I had never had that opportunity—and it's just one more thing I can do now. (Bergren, artists focus group interview)

Social Implications

Socially, all of the project participants—the coordinators, facilitators, artists, and students—learned a different form of communication through the creative process in an environment of free choice and mutual respect. By sharing

Figure: 2.3 Karen Willie Passey, teacher (right background), and *Snapshots* guest artist, Todd Newman (left foreground), introduce the next project to students and project facilitators.

personal stories, common interests, and struggles, both students and artists were able to better overcome their initial awkwardness with one another, as seen through the lens of social stereotyping—the *prima donna artist* and the *troubled youth*. With no one single authority, facilitators and artists served as guides during different phases of the project. Project facilitators navigated with the support of the students in an unfamiliar teaching/learning environment. Leaving behind roles such as those of generalist instructors, youth companions, teachers' aides, student intern, and counselor, all *assistants* unable to clearly visualize the end product were encouraged to trust in the nature of the project. Even *Snapshots'* coordinators were consistently challenged to trust in the more collaborative process.

While *Snapshots* was a structured project (with a syllabus, assignments, and basic parameters) it was neither hierarchical nor dictatorial. Coordinators, facilitators, artists, and students worked together collectively with each group having something to offer and learn from the other. Artists functioned as guides to the students, offering advice and direction when requested while emphasizing the students' free choice in creative decisions. This respect for the students' personal decision-making in choices of theme, text, and artistic composition, was illustrated by artist Surel Mitchell's observations regarding a difficult and recalcitrant student:

> The fact that she could do her own thing, and that it was okay to do her own thing, and she wasn't going to be told "no you can't do that," I think she opened up and really did an informative piece—it was great. (Mitchell, artists focus group interview)

Project facilitators associated with the primary partner organizations, the museum and school, were unknowingly subjected to a continuous team-building exercise. Trust and respect was created as shared goals became more evident and the development of common ground emerged through increased staff communication. Likewise artists and museum staff started to feel positive about working in the school environment, and trust was built between Work and Learn educators and community arts professionals. Everyone benefited and built trust through experience.

Interestingly, *Snapshots'* success was largely due to the interdependence of all its participants. While the two project coordinators organized the framework of *Snapshots* and served as leadership for the group (facilitators, artists, and students), they relied upon the artists to create the sample work for their art project and then to introduce it to students. Coordinators also depended upon facilitators to work with both artists and students to encourage the completion of each student's artwork. In turn, artists relied upon coordinators to structure and simplify their lesson and coordinate their materials. Work and Learn teachers depended upon coordinators and artists to organize and participate in each Friday afternoon session. While students typically look to teachers to lead the classroom, students participating in

Snapshots were often found assisting other students with their artwork. Thus, the *Snapshots* community, consisting of varying intergenerational players from diverse backgrounds labored communally toward the cumulative goal of creating a work of art for the final exhibition, and in the process, developed an elevated degree of trust and respect for all project participants.

This sense of community became evident in interviews with *Snapshots* participants. Work and Learn staff facilitators identified *Snapshots* as a form of "teambuilding" where all the staff of this small school worked toward a shared goal, learned to communicate better, and enjoyed working with one another in the process. As artist Karen Bubb observed, artists, facilitators, and students worked together and helped each other as if it were an *artist collective* based on partnerships *on all levels* rather than an authoritarian teacher/student learning hierarchy.

> [project coordinators] and the other teachers were going around helping all the kids and helping them develop their designs, and the kids were helping each other as well. So it was really like a little artist collective . . . very much based on partnerships both with all of the instructors and staff, as well as ourselves as artists, and the students. (Bubb, artists focus group interview)

Every year, youth were at first suspect, and then felt special and honored when artists and museum staff visited their *trailer*[4] repeatedly over the course of several months each year. In an environment of mutual respect and growing trust, both artists and students were able to share their personal stories, common interests, and vulnerabilities not only with each other but also with artists and the Boise community. Similar to the students, artists were asked to talk about their lives in relation to their artwork. As project coordinator, Passey described,

> Surel Mitchell . . . she really put herself on the line and talked about her own disability [multiple sclerosis], and because she opened herself up so much, I think other kids were then more willing to open up to her. (Passey, coordinators focus group interview)

Students and artists were pushed outside their *comfort zones*: students into their new, unfamiliar/inexperienced role as artists (perhaps grappling with the negative social stereotypes associated with artists), and artists into their role as teachers. Both groups were able to overcome the initial social awkwardness resulting from stereotyping and their generation gaps. Students' experiences with *Snapshots* provided insight into the lives of artists in their community. They learned that artists are real people and not the morose or elitist stereotypes characterized by the media. Students also expressed a desire to have more time to develop relationships with these artists conveying a sincere interest in working with and getting to know them better.

Psychological Implications

Themes of fear and uncertainty appeared to affect everyone in the beginning. Artists, students, and project facilitators were challenged to do something new, to work and explore outside of their *comfort zones*, and to take on new roles. Artists became teachers and learners. Students became artists and teachers. Project facilitators, who had no experience in teaching art, became art project leaders, assistants, and learners. In the end this temporary uneasiness among all participants led to the forming of extended support and concentric circles of community.

Figure: 2.4 Cameron Scott, *Dilemma*, 2003, encaustic and mixed-media on panel

"Dilemma . . . I want to be loyal to my friends but how I also want to do the right things . . . I have to make a lot of choices everyday, some easy, some hard, but I make these choices along with every other kid in the world."

Students considered tough questions. How do others see me? How do I see myself? Whom would I protect? What is my role in my family and home environment? Then, they created works that addressed these questions visually and in writing. An ongoing psychological investment and attachment to artmaking experiences and final products existed, exemplified by the fact that students knew exactly where their finished pieces would be today. Students also conveyed that those objects are highly valued by their keepers (themselves, family, and friends) much more so than other school products. Work and Learn student, Cameron, explained to researchers that his granddad gave him a drawing and then asked for one in return. By doing *Snapshots,* Cameron was able to exchange one of his artworks with his grandfather, further deepening their familial connection and common ground as artists. In perhaps one of the most clarifying moments of the reflection discussion with youth participants, Jessica, a 2-year student participant, relayed what she learned about life from working on *Snapshots* stating, "things aren't always the way you pictured them in your mind—but that you have to keep working, revising, working it out" (Jessica, students focus group interview.) Students in the group agreed that this serves as a description of and metaphor for life as well as the artistic processes encountered in the project.

Students experienced a surge in self-confidence as the different components of the project progressed, and especially during the final exhibition stage, where audience members talked with students about their feelings, artwork, and writing. They were also surprised that so many community members attended the exhibition reception, and as a result, began to recognize their own value in the community.

Artists mentioned preliminary fear and intimidation about working with youth, and in this case, disenfranchised youth. Insecurity about being misunderstood by teenagers, fear of having nothing to offer them, and not understanding what students might find interesting pervaded some artists' initial reactions to the project. Artists were also concerned with how they may potentially be perceived as *old, uncool,* or *boring*—exhibiting a lack of self-confidence when initially facing a younger audience. When asked about their first day experiences, Surel, a mature and well-established artist shared these concerns.

> [I felt] fear because I had never done anything like that before. I'm not a teacher. I had not a clue what I was going to do—I didn't know what to do so I walked in and just started talking to the kids like I had always been there . . . I wasn't being clear. [I felt] they didn't understand me. I felt like an idiot. (Mitchell, artists focus group interview)

Karen Bubb eloquently noted the youths' initial *testing attitude* for these new and strange adults in their midst.

> You would be looking at a group of 30 kids all packed into a room—sitting and looking at you [with arms folded as if to say] "What do you have to talk to me about?" Very reluctant—not thinking of themselves as artists—not

really thinking that you had anything to offer them directly, because they are not artists and they are not going to do your project anyway. So what I saw though over time—[was that] it was a defensiveness initially and that as we kept coming back—and I think part of it is figuring out that we aren't going to go away, and part of it is them—starting to work with them, their own materials and [them] becoming interested.

Once *Snapshots* began and initial layers of trust were built, youth became interested, invigorated and later empowered. Karen Bubb continues:

[Students later seemed to say] "Oh—maybe I can do this." . . . and they see their works on the walls . . . there was this pride of accomplishment . . . as they showed their friends or family or other people. So there was this real transformation that I saw was very visible in the kids [going] from the "I can't do that—I'm not an artist—who are you?" to this kind of excitement over this new possibility for them as people. (Bubb, focus group interview)

Artists also observed that they felt connected with the community in new ways and likewise experienced a rise in self-confidence.

I love being involved in the project. I love working in the community as an artist. It makes you feel like you are part of the community and gives you a lot of self-confidence, like "hey I can do something, aside from just staying by myself in my studio." (Bergren, focus group interview)

Significant Challenges

Students' lack of initial interest in the program was difficult to overcome. Building on repeat visits and experiences with one another, students and artists overcame their fears and the existing intergenerational challenges of skepticism, mistrust, and stereotypes of those older or younger than themselves. Coordinators now understand that incorporating more student involvement in planning and implementation (such as artist selection and/or endorsement of the project by the student council) will be crucial to future endeavors.

As all projects based in partnership are prone to do, *Snapshots'* level of equal partnership among individuals and entities waned periodically. Project facilitators were receivers to the coordinators already agreed upon project process, and consequently, were less invested as partners. Due to the involved nature of the project and territorial staff roles, buy-in from school and museum staff was difficult to cultivate. Later, too much buy-in was a challenge to balance and positively distill. Maintaining an equal level of vision, collaboration, and partnership among all entities was a challenge. Nonetheless, *Snapshots* was a rewarding experience and had something to offer every participant. For students and artists, the project taught participants a new method of expression through artmaking or teaching, while for project facilitators it introduced a new approach to teaching art (communal versus hierarchical), and illustrated art's potential for integration into other disciplines.

In the reflection discussion, Work and Learn staff did not seem to recognize *Snapshots'* potential as a template for further interdisciplinary projects involving art and academics at their school. In turn, however, they actively discussed the intense quickening and deepening levels of community within and outside of the school resulting from the project experience.

> You have to have this appreciation for working with youth whether you get to work on a project this grand or not. Most of the year, it's not grand, and you still have to have the appreciation for your kids or you're going to go crazy. I'd like to think the groups of colleagues I work with typically expect wonderful things from the kids every single day and not just for a grant that's been written. (Swanson, coordinators focus group interview)

Work and Learn teacher and project coordinator Karen Willie Passey clarifies,

> I think it's because we do respect our students, and we do know their talents and their abilities that we would even start a project like *Snapshots*. If we didn't think highly of them, why would we do something that takes a lot of extra time, energy, on all of us? We wouldn't do it. But we know our students are very talented and they have something to say to their community. (Passey, coordinators focus group interview)

Conclusion

Upon analyzing the reflection data, researchers discovered *Snapshots* initiated several intergenerational benefits including: (a) a heightened awareness of the role of informal mentorship, role modeling, and positive youth/adult relationship building in the lives of youth; (b) individual and collective experience within an intergenerational project; (c) re-connection of self with community; (d) empowerment for disenfranchised youth stemming from identity-related visual art and writing projects; (e) professional development opportunities for artists, arts professionals, and educators; and (f) an inventory of the important community connections facilitated by the project.

The evolving climate and educational vision of Work and Learn are integral to making projects like this successful. The willingness of art professionals to step outside their normal workplace roles is crucial to employing innovation and risk-taking in new educational programming. *Snapshots,* culling the combined efforts of project coordinators, Work and Learn, Boise Art Museum and the local community built an extended support system for students—and other participants—which continued to spiral outward becoming stronger and larger each year.

Furthermore, several of the characteristics proven helpful in educational success for all students and identified by the United States Department of Education (1998) such as setting high expectations, providing a safe learning environment, supporting students with extra help and time, and involving the community in schooling are found in *Snapshots.* As Barr and Parrett (2001) relay, "For at-risk youth, this community of support or *surrogate family* atmosphere, appears to be the single most important factor in assuring an at-risk student's academic success" (p. 67).

The normally occurring *surrogate family* atmosphere of Work and Learn School was intensified by the additional adult/youth relationships formed through the implementation of the project and evolving partnerships. Students met and worked with museum professionals, local artists, and a gallery owner and interacted with several audience members such as community members, artists, parents, and educators. All of these opportunities increased the self-confidence of every intergenerational participant and perceptions of their own value within the community. Spiraling further outward, year-by-year, layered circles of community evolved. Put simply, *Snapshots* could not have succeeded without the formation of concentric circles of community, as Passey further explains:

> The project couldn't happen without multiple levels of community . . . [there are] artists in the community who had their own projects that were great ideas to get us going . . . and the entire Work and Learn community which made sure that projects get finished . . . and the arts community—they are concentric circles of community all focused on this one group of kids, and that is a magical thing. If the world could be like this it would be a great thing—and you don't see it happening enough. (Passey, coordinators focus group interview)

References

Barr, R. D., & Parrett, W. H. (2001). *Hope fulfilled for at-risk and violent youth: K-12 programs that work* (2nd ed.). Allyn and Bacon: Boston.

United States Department of Education. *Turning around low-performing schools: A guide for state and local leaders*. (1998). Washington, DC: Author.

Endnotes

[1] The at-risk issues of these students go beyond school and the courts and include drug and alcohol addiction, abuse in their homes, depression, learning disabilities, and parents who are in prison or absent.

[2] Work and Learn, a unique secondary school sponsored by the Independent School District of Boise City, Ada County Juvenile Courts and the Hays Shelter, provides educational opportunities for 30 to 40 at-risk youth ages 14 to 18. Students are referred to the school because they are involved with juvenile courts, expelled or suspended from school, living at the Hays Shelter, or extremely depressed.

[3] Focus group interviews took place in December 2003: students, December 2 at the Work and Learn School; coordinators, December 8 at the Boise Art Museum; artists December 9 at the Boise Art Museum.; unpublished.

[4] In a self-deprecating term of endearment students occasionally refer to their school as a trailer because it is a modular building and looks similar to a trailer or mobile home.

3

Pamela Harris Lawton

Artstories©: Exploring Intergenerational Learning Connections Through Narrative Construction

> The community we achieve [through art], the dialogues we enter take shape across the differences, preventing those differences from tearing us apart, linking us in a desire to see more, understand more, listen more acutely, dip more passionately into life. (Greene, 2001, p. 148)

The decline of extended family networks that resulted in the *generation gap* has given rise to concerns regarding the social and moral education of children, the isolation of the older adult[1] and an increase in negative stereotypes and attitudes about both adolescence and aging. In an effort to address these concerns, government and community service organizations established intergenerational service learning programs that seek to connect youth with older adults through educational and creative activities that benefit each generation. There are three types of intergenerational service learning programs: youth serving seniors,

seniors serving youth, and reciprocal or mutual programs where no one group serves another, but each works cooperatively as a team sharing responsibilities and benefits (Perlstein & Bliss, 1994). Of the three, reciprocal programs have the highest success record.

This chapter discusses the results and implications of an epistemological action research study of an age-integrated, reciprocal arts learning program. The study, entitled *Artstories©*, examined the nature of the learning and social relationships that evolved among three generations of women and girls previously unknown to one another working together on a collaborative visual and verbal narrative based in their lived experiences. *Artstories* was designed to (a) emulate the creative learning environment of extended family networks, (b) foster social, moral and arts learning, and (c) generate a sense of community among two or more generations of participants.

I originally coined the term *Artstories*, to describe my own art process, visual/verbal narratives in the form of prints, assemblages, and artist books that preserve and reinterpret family history and intergenerational relationships. In this context, *Artstories* was used to describe the process of combining oral, written, and visual narrative into artist books representative of a multiplicity of generational voices on issues related to the coming of age within a multicultural society and those common rites of passage associated with being in and passing through adolescence. Through this study the *Artstories* concept expanded from the individual and personal (my own art making process) to the collective and general (intergenerational group collaboration).

The Art of Storytelling

For as long as I can remember I have had a love affair with stories: listening to, reading, writing, drawing, telling, and singing them. Those within my sphere of influence having the greatest impact on my own self-narratives were my sister, parents, grandmother, and great-aunt. As an adult reminiscing upon my memories of familial interaction, my recall of certain incidents is restructured, altering time, so that they occur sequentially as opposed to randomly. These memories often converge and meld together as one lengthy event, similar to the following excerpts from my *Artstory*, "Little Turtles."

> Of course I do not remember that first meeting with my sister, but she does and she describes it so vividly that it is etched within my own mind along side memories that I do recall—like a scene from a favorite TV sitcom rerun so many times that image, action and dialogue permeate my brain, tangling up with first-hand recollections.

We met 44 years ago on a cold, clear January day—the last day of the first week of the first month of the last year of the decade. She had waited patiently, for six years, enjoying all the attention lavished upon her, but anxious for someone of her very own to share it with. These last nine months had been the hardest, not because their attention was shifting from her, but because they didn't listen to her anymore, they didn't believe her when she said it would be a girl. She prayed—God listened.

Mama was seated in great-grandma's rocking chair, Daddy standing by her side, when she was finally allowed into the room. They were both smiling at the small bundle wiggling in Mama's arms. She rushed in jumping, bouncing like the little ball she used to play jacks with, unable to contain her excitement as she peered at the tiny red face buried in the bundle.

"Oh, can I hold her? Can I? Can I?" Words tumbling so fast they tripped over one another in their rush to be said. "Shh! Don't move around so much, you'll scare the baby!" The joy that had bubbled up like the fragile iridescent beauties she created with her bubble wand plopped down on the hardwood floor in a wet splash as the corners of her mouth drooped, her bottom lip quivered, and tears swam in her eyes. Slowly she turned and walked dejectedly towards the door.

"Wait! Come back!" She obeyed, a tentative smile playing upon her lips as she slowly walked back towards them, noting their astonished expressions. "I don't believe it. She shouldn't be able to focus yet." Sensing a kindred spirit, I had looked into my big sister's face—eyes following her as she made to leave, following her as she came back. It was love at first sight. The beginning of a relationship unrivaled, untouched, unchanged, and unfathomable.

The new bedroom furniture had arrived that morning and we eagerly helped Mama and Daddy put our clothes away in pungent smelling cedar drawers. The room was so much bigger now without the two beds side by side. Of course we both wanted the top bunk, but Marsha vetoed, being the oldest she had first dibs. I could tell that the three of them were also afraid that I might somehow manage to roll off the edge in my sleep and crash to the floor, in spite of the guardrail designed to prevent such an accident.

For once we were not anxious to run outside after dinner and play with our friends. Instead we went back to our room, a new and different place. We each had a desk and bookshelf complete with "junk drawers." I carefully placed my treasures—rocks and shells gathered from the woods next to our house and vacations at the beach, coins from places I'd never been but hoped to one day see and placed them in the little drawers as Marsha lined the book shelves with her favorite books, pausing to set aside one that she'd checked out of the library after school on Friday.

Dum-da-dee-dum-da-dee-dum-da-dee-dum-da-dee-dum-dum, as the Cartwrights rode off into the sunset toward the Ponderosa we marched upstairs to our new beds. Hugs, and soft kisses, darkness, footsteps receding down the hallway—whispered words, "Pam, are you ready?" "Uh huh." Marsha had arranged her blanket so that only one edge of it was tucked beneath her mattress—on the same side where the guardrail she had shoved under my bed was supposed to be. She pushed the blanket so that it completely covered the side of my bed. As she gingerly climbed down the ladder she pulled her bedspread, tucked in at the foot of the mattress, down—completely enclosing us in a tent formed by the bedclothes, wall and top bunk.

It was a new and exciting twist to our favorite and oldest game. She squeezed in next to me and retrieved the pen flashlight and book, "The Lion, the Witch, and the Wardrobe," she had hidden under my pillow earlier that day. The muffled sound of girlish giggles rose up from the mound of covers as we squiggled to pull the edge of the spread over our backs so that it rested just at the juncture of our heads and necks—two little turtles— sisters, so close that they shared the same shell. (*Little Turtles*, Lawton, 2001)

Storytelling in all of its forms: oral, visual, written, and performed, is a vital component of our lives from the time we enter the world until we leave it. As such narratives infiltrate all facets of daily existence from family and peer interaction to school and work life. Narrative imagination is pivotal to the maturation process. Fiction, folklore, stories of our experiences and tales shared by the people within our sphere of influence intertwine, teaching us about family, culture, heritage, traditions and those behaviors deemed *socially acceptable*.

Stories educate even as they entertain, and everyone has a story to share, as well as one they want to hear. Stories help envision dreams and set goals for what we hope to accomplish in life. As toddlers we learn the concept of story, the real from the imagined, and we begin to borrow the conventions of storytelling to create self-narratives, richly textured tales that combine memory and imagination. And, we learn how to manipulate these stories to our advantage (Bettleheim, 1976; Bruner, 2002; Pradl, 1984). As we embellish our self-narratives enriching real-life experience with tales that inspire us and fire the imagination, we sculpt and shape our self-identities, constantly refining an artwork that is never quite finished. Once an experience has been lived it cannot be completely or faithfully re-created in any form exactly as it originally occurred (Riessman, 1993). Therefore each re-presentation of an experience is unique and has its own interpretation, however subtle, making it more akin to *lived fiction* rather than absolute truth.

Crossing Boundaries and Bridging Generations Through the Art of Story Making

To be effective and meaningful on any level, verbal, visual or written, communication must kindle a spark of interest to initiate a connection. Oral story sharing coaxes strangers into conversation with one another. Story sharing aids in the transfer of values and history from one generation to the next, building a bridge that spans the age barrier. It is also a means of self-making, a form of self-identity construction through the retelling and reinterpretation of memories recycled and reformed throughout life.

Yet, how does narrative artmaking aid in the establishment of an intergenerational connection? Recalling memories, reflecting upon them, and using this knowledge to plan future actions is an inherently human characteristic (Smith-Shank & Schwiebert, 2000). Everyone has the capacity to form mental images or visual representations of memorable life events that, like a favorite film, remain sharp and clear in our mind's eye over the course of time. These mental pictures are transformed into narratives, shared with unrelated others, and put to paper in the form of artist books that may be used as a credible means of connecting people, particularly people of different generations.

Narrative forms of expression—oral, written, visual, and performed—once united generations of family and transmitted the learning of moral values, social mores, family traditions, history and culture. Because the American family dynamic has shifted over the last century, from extended family networks to a nuclear family structure, those intergenerational *teachable* moments which once occurred at home with family, close friends and neighbors, now need to be orchestrated by schools and community programs.

Artstories was modeled after successful reciprocal intergenerational programs like ESTA[2] and City Lore[3] where participants from arts agencies, neighborhood senior centers, and schools have an equal voice in program planning and decision making. Each participant shares their family histories as the basis of collaborative works of art, e.g., plays, poems, and artworks, thus, learning about each other's culture and traditions. The end result is displayed or performed in a public art space. This process allows participants to reach out to one another as well as others within the community. *Artstories* seeks to bring the learning

33

potential of successful programs like these into the classroom. Many of the most effective educational experiences are those that involve the community in some way and have a direct application to life beyond school.

An Empowering Event

The *Artstories* study was designed to encourage a transformative learning experience through the art of story making. "Transformative learning occurs when, through critical self-reflection, an individual revises old or develops new assumptions, beliefs or ways of seeing the world" (Cranton, 1994, p. xii). In transformative learning theory, attitudes and beliefs are referred to as *meaning perspectives*. Meaning perspectives develop during the socialization process in childhood and "refer to the structure of assumptions within which new experience is assimilated and transformed by one's past experience during the process of interpretation" (Mezirow, 1990, p. 2).

The process of transforming meaning perspectives is referred to as *perspective transformation*. Through perspective transformation we become critically aware of our assumptions and how we feel, think, and see the world. We become open to changing the habitual structures that guide our thoughts and actions seeking a more integrative perspective and making new life choices using these new understandings (Mezirow, 1991). Learners must be empowered first, before critical self-reflection can take place, and conversely, empowerment increases critical self-reflection (Cranton, 1994). The act of narrating, recounting memories of lived experience and the learning that occurred, as well as listening to the stories of others different from the self, is a naturally self-reflective process. Experiences drive critical self-reflection of assumptions. Sharing experiences through group discussion and hands-on activity promotes personal reflection and the reconstruction of meaning. Within a small group setting like *Artstories*, this process may give rise to belief and attitude change. Through the sharing of individual narratives and the collective creation of oral, written, and visual narratives based in lived experiences, *Artstories* allowed participants to become involved in an *empowering event*. The *Artstories* created by the participants were then shared with others in their community promoting intergenerational understanding, empathy, and cohesion.

"Through stories people see connections—connections among their experiences and the experiences of others, and connections between experience and underlying social values. Recognizing these connections is essential in developing empowerment" (Barakett & Sacca, 2002, p. 44).

34

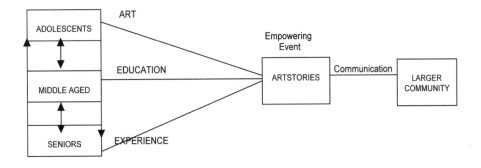

Figure: 3.1. Artstories as Empowering Event

The *Artstories* Story

My teaching experience and arts practice led me to question the transformative learning potential of intergenerational interaction and how narrative art making promotes and enhances social and moral learning among two or more generations of strangers. Observing my students, senior volunteers in the school, and my family members, and reflecting upon my own stories of growing up and my art making interests led to several research questions: (a) Can a three-pronged approach (oral, written, and visual) to the creation of a collective narrative among intergenerational, multi-ethnic groups of strangers lead to perspective transformation regarding moral and social issues and perceptions concerning age, culture, and ethnicity?; (b) Does the act of constructing a collective narrative based upon participants' lived experiences lead to empowerment and promote social as well as personal transformation? And if so, how might schools, arts and community service organizations partner to develop curricula and programs to promote transformative learning and generate community?

Given these considerations, the study needed to take place within a community setting conducive to arts learning, where several generations were likely to meet and mingle comfortably. In order for *Artstories* to work as a curriculum model, the design needed to be flexible and adaptable to classrooms and community centers as well as the family gatherings upon which it is based. Therefore, three of the four *Artstories* case studies were conducted in the art room at the Goddard-Riverside Community Center (GRCC) in New York City. I selected this senior center because it is located in a diverse community and the majority of the center's senior members live alone and have little or no contact with family members, making them an ideal population for inclusion in *Artstories,* partnering two or more generations of people with little or no access to their own extended family. In addition the center offers programs that span the generational spectrum including partnerships with three public schools. The fourth study, conducted with my own family, took place in my mother's home.

Each case study was conducted over a three-week period for three hours each week. Participants were volunteers with an interest in artmaking from GRCC, Teachers College, and two local high schools, Heritage High School[4] and the Renaissance Charter High School[5]. The ages of participants ranged from 14 to 82 and spanned four racial groups and several ethnicities. Each case study was conducted in the same manner. I began by introducing myself and explaining the purpose of the study. I then gave each participant a pre-activity questionnaire with ten questions to complete. The questions were designed to find out partici-pants' feelings about stories, whether or not people learn from stories, how they felt about sharing their own stories, and whether or not they had regular contact with family members or friends outside of their own generation. Next, to ease tension, I told a story from my own childhood. Then, I asked each person seated at the table to share a personal story with the group. This helped them get to know one another and be more comfortable working together. The large group was then divided into smaller groups comprising more than one generation each. Group C was an exception, as there were only two adolescents, the group remained one large group of nine. Each group was then asked to compose a story together, one with a beginning, middle, and end that would combine their collective experiences into one narrative. What would the story be about? How would they begin it? How would it end? Each person had to contribute to the narrative and each group selected a scribe to write the story down. All partici-pated in the shaping of their story. Each person in each group also needed to contribute illustrations to their story. Everyone elected to illustrate their part of the story and copies of their illustrations were made for everyone in their group.

Thus *Artstories* began as an oral process that was then written as a story and illustrated. The latter half of the first session was spent showing the groups how to make decorative papers with marbling and paste paper techniques. Creating these decorative pieces to be used for their books deepened the connections that began to form as each person took a very active interest in the designs, patterns and decora-tions their fellow participants were creating. At the close of the first session, homework was given out. Each person was to illustrate their part of the story (photocopies were made at the center for each person), and the scribe's job was to type up the story. Copies of each story were then given to each member of the group.

During session two, participants were shown three different handmade book formats and asked to choose one for their story. The idea was for each participant to walk away from the study with their own book containing their collective story and illustrations. In addition, each person had the freedom to design their book covers and negative space areas as they pleased, making the book both a group and an individual art piece. Once the book format was chosen each person was responsible for constructing their book with the group deciding on the layout of text and image. The final session was spent putting the finishing touches to the books and having a *show and tell* session. In addition a ten-question post-activity questionnaire was handed out, with a self-addressed, stamped envelope to elicit participants' responses regarding the experience. Were they now more or less interested in sharing stories with others? How did they feel about collaborating on a story? Did they learn anything new or different about life and people as a result of creating a shared story with people they did not know of different ages and cultural backgrounds?

As the researcher, I received a book from each group. Each session was videotaped, and I took copious field and journal notes. In-depth video interviews were conducted with each member of Group C. I was an active participant in Groups C and D. These two studies took place in July and August of 2002 respectively. I did not participate in Groups A and B. The latter two studies took place simultaneously in July 2001. Data collection consisted of primary data sources: (a) anecdotal records on individual behavior episodes; (b) field notes covering group interactional episodes; (c) observational notes encompassing direct listening and watching; (d) procedural field notes which covered my decision-making strategies as participant/researcher in an action research study; (e) interview field notes containing views, ideas, and actions; (f) journal notes, used as evidence for change related to including the middle generation in the study (not my initial intent); and (g) audiovisual records of events and the *Artstory* artifacts (completed books) as narrative evidence. The only secondary data collection methods employed were the pre-and post-activity questionnaires used to examine participants' views and responses.

Artstories data was filtered through Clandinin and Connelly's (2000) *three-dimensional metaphoric framework*, based in Dewey's definition and conception of experience as education. Dimension One is the personal and social, Dewey's *interaction*. Dimension Two is the temporal—past, present and future, Dewey's *continuity*. Dimension Three is place, Dewey's *situation*—the boundaries, tangible and topological within which inquiry occurs. Within these dimensions, the researcher, in a participatory action research study like this one, moves in four different directions: inward, examining internal feelings, emotions, and oral dispositions; outward, investigating the surrounding environment; and backward and forward, exploring temporality—past, present and future (Clandinin & Connelly, 2000).

This metaphorical narrative framework was ideal for evaluating *Artstories* where participants created a collective narrative encompassing the personal and social across time (temporal) to establish a learning connection among members of a particular community (place). Story is the *unit of analysis* in narrative inquiry, and the goal is to make meaning through storied examination of lived experience (Clandinin & Connelly, 2000).

Three data analysis strategies were employed. At the broadest level, data was analyzed through the cyclical participatory action research model of plan, act, observe, reflect, and revise. As reflected in observations and field notes at the end of each session, the plan for the next session was reviewed to implement

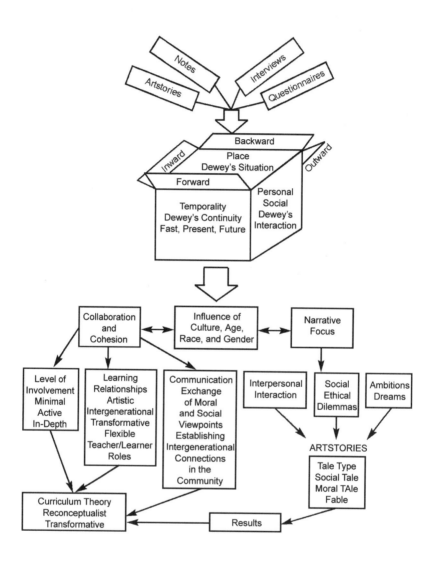

Figure: 3.2. Data Analysis Flowchart

38

improvements extracted from data analysis. This shifting back and forth between "concrete pieces of data, abstract concepts, inductive/deductive reasoning and description and interpretation" (Merriam, 1998, p. 178) guided the next level of data analysis: analytic induction. Analytic induction is a form of thematic analysis whereby the research identifies specific themes and categories that are interpreted in relation to the research questions posed. The themes that arose from analytic induction resulted from evaluating the data through Clandinin and Connelly's narrative framework. These themes were then further reduced into categories and strands from which meaning criteria were established. The three dominant themes which emerged from *Artstories* were: (a) collaboration and cohesion among participants; (b) influence of culture, age, and race; and (c) narrative focus. Within the themes, categories and strands were identified that further detailed and shaped *Artstories*. Each of the categories and strands directly related to the type of tale groups elected to tell: moral, social, fable, or any combination thereof.

Theme one, collaboration and cohesion among participants, describes individual and group interaction and behavior in terms of the level of involvement, learning relationships, and communication. Level of involvement was characterized as minimal, active or in-depth and refers to individual interaction within a group. If rapport among participants in a given group was strong, then their interaction with one another was more involved. Learning relationships were divided into four sub-themes: artistic learning, intergenerational learning, transformative learning, and flexible teacher/learner roles. Each described the learning that took place. For example, everyone learned artistically as no one had experience making artist's books. The category communication refers to communicating *Artstories* learning with others outside of the study, which was one of the goals, to take what was learned and share it within the community.

Theme two, influence of culture, race and age, examines theme one, collaboration and cohesion, which speaks to the nature of the group dynamic, through the lens of the participant's culture, race and age. Theme three, narrative focus was divided into three sub-themes: interpersonal interactions, social and ethical dilemmas, and ambitions and dreams. This theme mirrors group discussion and interaction. The categories refer to the focus that influenced group discourse. These sub-themes were further divided into *tale types*, the type of tale each group elected to tell fell into one of three types or a combination thereof: moral, social, and fable or fairy tale.

Moral tales were stories about ethical and social dilemmas that face us as young adolescents and adults and close with a moral or lesson to be learned. Social tales encompassed stories about interpersonal interaction, such as relationships with the opposite sex. Fables were fictional stories about the realization of personal ambitions, goals, and dreams. Additionally the *Artstories* were written

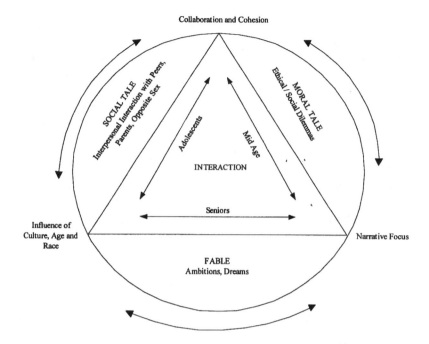

Figure: 3.3. Artstories Themes

using three different formats: combined character, multiple characters, and the add-on story. Combined character stories revolved around one composite character, a combination of the experiences and stories of all the participants in the group. In multiple character stories, each participant is a character within the story and the story itself is a combination of all the participants' stories in one composite story. With the add-on story one person creates the beginning of the story and each person adds to it with the last person supplying the ending. The add-on story also revolved around one central character.

In considering what needed to occur for the study to be meaningful, the following meaning criteria were established: (a) development of a rapport with another generation, (b) sharing of and discussion about moral/social viewpoints through narrative arts learning, (c) critical review and possible revision of previously held assumptions, and (d) sharing the intergenerational learning experience culled within the group with at least one person outside of the study. If at least three of these criteria were met, so was the goal of the research and the results were considered meaningful. Therefore, at the low end of the continuum, results were meaningful if participants were receptive to and interacted with participants of different ages. At the high end of the continuum, results were meaningful if participants critically reviewed and revised their meaning perspectives (transformative learning) as a direct result of intergenerational interaction.

Examination of Results by Theme, Tale Type and Meaning Criteria

Themes and Strands	Group A	Group B	Group C	Group D
Collaboration & Cohesion				
Level of Intergenerational Involvement	Active	In-depth	Minimal	In-depth
Learning Relationships	Artistic learning Flexible role play	Transformative learning Flexible role play Intergenerational understanding	Artistic learning Intergenerational understanding	Artistic learning Intergenerational understanding Transformative learning
Communication	Exchange of moral/social views Connections to the larger community	Exchange of moral/social views Connections to the larger community	Exchange of moral/social views	Exchange of moral/social views Connection to other family members
Influence of Age, Race, Culture & Gender	Culture	Gender	Race Culture	Age
Narrative Focus **Tale Type**	Moral	Social	Fable	Social and Moral
*Meaning Criteria (1-4)	1,2,3 and 4	1,2,3 and 4	1, 3 and 4	1,2,3, and 4

1. Development of a rapport with another generation.
2. Sharing of and discussion about moral/social viewpoints through narrative arts learning.
3. Critical review and possible revision of previously held assumptions.
4. Sharing the intergenerational learning experience culled within the group with at least one person outside of the study.

Figure: 3.4. Data Analysis Flowchart

Results

Findings indicated that the seniors felt it important to praise the teens and encourage them in their creativity. The teens felt it was important to listen to and support the seniors' wisdom and ideas. Those in the middle generation were impelled to cement the tenuous bond that developed by reminiscing on their own youth and relationships with older family members. Within each group there was an atmosphere of caring, of *watching out* for one another. This caring was manifested through listening to and helping one another in each stage of the *Artstories* project and is evident in the artifacts that were created. Several of the teens transformed their perceptions regarding seniors and their understanding of the growing pains adolescents experience in the process of becoming responsible adults. All left the project with a feeling of empowerment, having connected with someone different, and created an artifact of personal and social significance to share with someone else.

Summary

As researcher/participant I reflected upon what *Artstories* accomplished, the impetus for the study, results, inferences drawn, and the implications for art teachers, schools, and communities, and found the need for an age-integrated arts learning curriculum theory. Based in a reconceptualist curriculum ideology, an age integrated arts learning curriculum theory would embrace the autobiographical experiences of the students, their artistic interests, the literature that influences their perceptions and actions, and the social and moral issues that drive their critical consciousness, thus, allowing them to make connections through art, writing, and personal lived experience to the school and the broader community.

There are several ways in which schools can expand their curriculum to include the broader community through age-integrated arts/language learning activities. As a first step, Gillis (1992) suggests a classroom activity that allows students to discuss their thoughts and attitudes concerning the aged and aging, examine where their attitudes come from, and determine whether they are based in fact or fiction. Similarly, I would suggest that students then take on the role of an older person and answer these same questions with adolescence as the subject. This gives students a clearer picture of age prejudice and prepares them to begin challenging their own assumptions, paving the way for a transformative learning experience. Students could then conduct some field research interviewing seniors and their families and community. The lesson could continue with writing prompts around photographs or drawings of seniors or non-biased statements about aging. A field trip to the senior center could be arranged. All of these could be preliminary activities leading to an *Artstories* project.

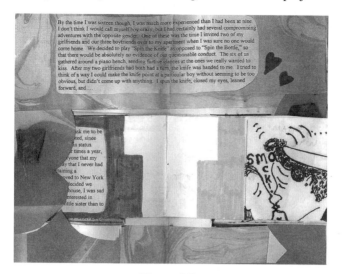

Figure: 3.5

Education is about life; life is an education. From beginning to end life is a journey of self-discovery; and the adventures and travelers we encounter along the road become key coordinates on our memory map. These informal learning experiences in conjunction with our formal schooling comprise our education and influence the teachings we pass on to others through the sharing of life stories.

She told him that every time she went to the park without her mother's permission, she would always get hurt. We hoped he would take this as a lesson and learn that misbehavior has its consequences.

One day Valentina and I took him to the park where we met Gretel. She told us one of her stories. When she lived in Germany, she and two of her friends wanted to try smoking.

Figure: 3.6

References

Barakett, J., & Sacca, E. (2002). Narratives empowering teachers and students: Educational practice. In Y. Gaudelius & P. Speirs (Eds), *Contemporary issues in art education.* New Jersey: Prentice Hall.

Bettleheim, B. (1976). *The uses of enchantment: The meaning and importance of fairy tales.* New York: Alfred Knopf.

Bruner, J. (2002). *Making stories: Law, literature, life.* New York: Farrar, Strauss & Giroux.

Clandinin, D. J., & Connelly, F. M. (2000). *Narrative inquiry: Experience and story in qualitative research.* San Francisco: Jossey-Bass.

Cranton, P. (1994). *Understanding and promoting transformative learning: A guide for educators of adults.* San Francisco: Jossey-Bass.

Gillis, C. (1992). *The community as classroom: Integrating school and community through language arts.* Portsmouth, NH: Boyton/Cook.

Greene, M. (2001). *Variations on a blue guitar: The Lincoln Center Institute lectures on aesthetic education.* New York: Teachers College Press.

Lawton, P. H. (2001). *Little Turtles.* Unpublished manuscript.

Lawton, P. H. (2004). *Artstories©: Perspectives on intergenerational learning through narrative construction amongst adolescents, middle aged and older aged adults.* Unpublished doctoral dissertation. Teachers College Columbia University, New York.

Merriam, S. B. (1998). *Case study research in education: A qualitative approach.* San Francisco: Jossey-Bass.

Mezirow, J. (1990). *Fostering critical reflection in adulthood.* San Francisco: Jossey-Bass.

Mezirow, J. (1991). *Transformative dimensions of adult learning.* San Francisco: Jossey-Bass.

Perlstein, S., & Bliss, J. (1994). *Generating community: Intergenerational partnerships through the expressive arts.* New York: The Print Center.

Pradl, G. (1984). *Narratology: The study of story structure.* Illinois: Office of Educational Research and Improvement, United States Department of Education. (ERIC Document Reproduction Service No. ED250698)

Riessman, C. K. (1993). *Narrative analysis.* Newbury Park, CA: Sage.

Smith-Shank, D., & Schwiebert, V. (2000). Old wives' tales: Questing to understand visual memories. *Studies in Art Education, 19*(3), 37-47.

Endnotes

[1] For the purposes of this study, an older adult or senior is a person 55 years of age or older, the age at which most people are eligible for retirement.

[2] ESTA is a community arts organization that was founded in 1979 in New York City. The staff is composed of professional educators, social workers and artists who work with the old and the young in various communities throughout New York City and beyond to foster intergenerational, intercultural connections through the arts (Perlstein & Bliss, 1994).

[3] City Lore, established in 1986, is a non-profit membership organization that specializes in building connections between local and national cultural resources and K-12 educational programs. Their staff is comprised of folklorists, anthropologists, and ethnomusicologists who create programs and materials for public and educational enjoyment (www.citylore.com).

[4] The Heritage School is a collaboration between Teachers College Columbia University and the New York City Board of Education. It is located in East Harlem in the Julia de Burgos Latino Cultural Center and integrates the arts into both the school day and the extended day curriculum.

[5] The Renaissance Charter School is a K-12 school of 500 students in the Bronx, New York that provides an intimate, caring, and diverse community of staff and parents dedicated to developing students' leadership skills.

4

Erin Tapley

Seniors With Cognitive Disabilities: Assisting Visual Memory

This chapter is a case study of how an intergenerational art program, Project A.R.T. (Art as Recreational Therapy), seemed to influence the memory recall and art of cognitively disabled adults during a weekly art course at the University of Wisconsin at Oshkosh. Now in its fourth year and eighth semester, directed and taught by the university art education faculty with assistance from university student volunteers, 60 Oshkosh citizens, and members of A.R.C. (Advocating for the Rights and Choices of Persons with Disabilities) participated. The A.R.C. and local sponsorship donated funding for the materials, some transportation, and the annual art exhibition. Older adults in Project A.R.T. comprised about 30-percent of the whole student body. These persons have had extensive childhood art experiences and comprised a growing subset of the older adult population "as improved health care has allowed them unprecedented longevity" (Tingey, 1988, p. 344). One distinct feature of this group, however, was that long-term recall was slow and/or sporadic or sometimes non-existent. I believe that they have been often environmentally encouraged to think and speak about short-term events or pragmatic daily tasks. Reflection about the *distant past,* especially during recreational activities with non-family members, was uncommon.

Figure 4.1 A night at Project A.R.T.

Four seniors with cognitive disabilities successfully recalled and expressed childhood memories through visual memory projects with the assistance of young university students who interviewed seniors, listened to their stories, and shared their own. The triangulation of data in the form of university student journals, the content of memory projects, observations and senior artists' biographical information revealed evidence of this phenomenon.

About the Memory Projects

Memory projects were initially designed and proposed in an attempt to inspire greater reflection and imagination from all of the artists in Project A.R.T. As the four-year director of this program, I felt that too often, when left to whim, subject matter in our art classes veered toward repetitive conventions. In other words, artists would make images or sculpt symbols of upcoming holidays such as Valentine's Day hearts or hobbies/obsessions such as the Green Bay Packer helmets or video game characters. While I don't believe there is anything wrong with such subject matter, I felt the immediacy with which students called upon these ideas stifled their thoughtfulness and often led to rushed, unchallenging, dead-end art. I contemplated the conundrum of inability versus inexperience: Were repetitive artistic behaviors learned or therapeutic? How could I enable students to have and use new ideas? Finally, I experimented with changing the entire thrust of the class. I encouraged autobiographical substance for creating art and I would frame each class by asking a relevant question about their lives: "What is your favorite meal?" and "Can you draw a map to show how you get from your house to Project A.R.T.?" I also tried to inspire the artist with slides, posters, or even short video clips of artists who had depicted similar things. In essence, I taught the class at a university level using a more structured studio approach with stimulating content rather than introducing art media or methods and asking students to make anything—which often led to simplified clichés, such as, love represented by a heart or spring by a flower.

While I cannot claim that every student was always able or willing to focus on these autobiographical and thought-provoking frameworks, the process of creating with a new attitude piqued interest, and there was more discussion between older adult students and their university student assistants. Then, after reading some university student journals one night, I uncovered their curiosity about the older adults' earlier lives. I realized that "childhoods," although they would certainly be different, were a common factor that we could all discuss and hopefully express. I devised three projects that I hoped would help all participants learn about each other's young lives. These were presented as follows:

1. **Childhood Toy:** What was your favorite childhood toy? Do you remember when you got it—was it for Christmas or a birthday? What did it look like? Do you still have it? Where did you play with it?

(Students were shown a toy from my past and asked to visualize one from their own. Multicolored Model Magic was then used to try and sculpt their toy. Artists were then asked to paint a background for the toy as the context of where they used it.)

2. **Map of House:** When you were a kid, where was your favorite place to go? Was it to the library, the ice cream parlor, the playground, etc.? How far was this from your house? Do you remember the route you took to get there? Can you draw a map of that route?

(Students were shown cartographic works by Hundertwasser, Aboriginal artists, and David Hockney. They were then asked to use a 2D media and paper and encouraged to depict a kind of aerial map of this subject. University student volunteers were asked to record an explanation about the map on the back of each picture.)

3. **The Best Thing About Oshkosh:** Since Oshkosh was celebrating its 150th anniversary, there were many related events and available literature. Most Project A.R.T. students were born in Oshkosh or lived there for a significantly long time.

(Students were asked to think about the 150th anniversary. Posters were shown, and we guessed the locations in some old photographs. Students were then instructed to draw or sculpt the best thing about Oshkosh.)

How Do Disabilities Affect the Expressive Abilities of the Studied Artists?

While there was a range of motor and cognitive abilities among the four senior citizens described in this paper, all were able to speak and direct their drawing or sculpting into a theme with occasional prompting. In comparison to my work with non-cognitively disabled seniors, those in this study were encouraged to make art recreationally throughout their lives and demonstrated a greater facility and enthusiasm in the start up processes. On the other hand, self-perception seems to differ greatly between the two groups. In my experiences in creating art with healthy or typical senior populations, I've noticed that many grasp their past experiences, their retirement, and perhaps weakening physicality as evidence of "getting up there" in age. The cognitively disabled seniors in my study did not seem to exhibit or discuss such self-perception. All have retired from working in a factory type job for a few hours a day, but none were cognizant of salary or money. The seniors did occasionally mention their decreased agility or stamina. I've also known each one of them to celebrate their birthday with much anticipation and complete gusto. All of them have experienced the death of both parental guardians, but have cited siblings or younger relatives as those who were taking care of them now. In one case the senior Project A.R.T. student referred to a guardian niece as "mom." I am not implying that life was completely dandy and worried free for the senior subjects of this paper, but they do not seem to partition their lives based on literal age, employment, or even family position. To them, more meaningful connections seemed to be made when settings and people were recalled. Additionally, each of them seemed decisively happy. If something "sad" came up in our conversations, all would shift gears and conjure more positive events. (e.g., "My mother died last year, but I still got my sister and she's coming over in August"). After the September 11th tragedy when many university students were creating memorial drawings, I also noticed that none of the Project A.R.T. seniors were so inclined. Birthdays, holidays, and seasonal images predominated their "freestyle" drawing subjects.

Student Volunteers' Perceptions of Working with the Project A.R.T. Seniors

A primary objective of university student volunteers, predominantly education majors in Project A.R.T., was to gain experience interacting with exceptional learners for future application in their own teaching. In their journals, they regularly described their perceptions of the working processes of older persons in our class, which I also confirmed as trends through observation and group meetings with all of the project A.R.T. volunteers. Conclusions found through triangulation of the data were that older adult students: (a) preferred to make art for people rather than just for themselves or for fun; (b) demonstrated strong idiosyncratic ways of making things such as trees, houses, and flowers, which seemed to be from childhood schemas; (c) laughed more, talked more, and were less restless than the university student assistants; (d) were never resistant about trying something new, however tended to accept first-time results as final; (e) had a slower mode of working than younger student counterparts; (f) tended to be more aware of using all of the clay, using the whole piece of drawing paper, being sure all of the markers had caps on them, etc.; and (g) were more influenced by examples presented around the room than younger university student assistants.

Students' Self-Assessment of Their Interaction with Project A.R.T. Seniors

Because the subjects of this chapter are the seniors and 12 young student assistants, I watched and listened to their responses and interactions. I also excerpted remarks from the university students' journals describing common moments in working on the memory projects with Project A.R.T.

1. University student volunteers experienced initial doubt with regard to the memory projects because they thought rudimentary conversation was difficult enough, and they were not sure if the older students would want to "look back."

2. University student volunteers discovered that they must create ways to indicate the idea of "a long time ago in your past" for some Project A.R.T. seniors. They attempted to do this by bringing out a relative's baby photograph from their wallets. The sharing of pictures particularly seemed to delight the Project A.R.T. students.

3. Images, i.e., street maps from the telephone book, seemed like a good idea to jumpstart the communication necessary to begin the projects.

4. It took the university student volunteers longer to feel comfortable with their older partners. Volunteers expressed uncertainty as to whether to perceive/treat them as stately wise folks or to be more nurturing.

Quotes from the university volunteer journals confirmed that the cognitively disabled students were able to remember and discuss more about their remote past than originally expected and apply it to their art.

I didn't think that this population would remember much about their younger years but they do and it is really stirring to think that little things such as a Christmas present can stay with you your whole life and maybe even stand for who you are. (volunteer journal)

It was a good idea to do projects about their early lives, because I noticed that some of them would then think to ask us questions about our own childhoods and this led to a lot of joking around. You also start to realize that a lot of the (Project A.R.T.) seniors never really grew up. For example, when I was talking about the Care Bears and other early 1980s toys I had, they told me that they had these too and drew them accurately—my own grandparents wouldn't have a clue about these things. (volunteer journal)

Because these people are pretty up on Oshkosh and have lived here most of their lives they're pretty attached. They don't know historical details, but they'll talk about stuff like the baseball fields or the lake flies or a relative receiving a fishing trophy or something. (volunteer journal)

My own observations of each cognitively disabled student were very similar to those found in the university student journals.

Susan

Susan was our oldest class member at age 71. She looked frail and drew delicately but she had never missed an art class in three years. Susan now lives with a niece and her children to whom she has transferred the role of mom and siblings. She maintains a cozy lifestyle of reading books, copying texts from books (she refers to as "doing her homework"), watching TV, taking short neighborhood walks and participating in gentle activities with her new family. Susan's favorite subject also happens to be Oshkosh, where she has spent much of her life. The absolutely correct details of Susan's responses needed some editing from her relatives, but Susan did seem to understand the essence of each of the memory projects.

Susan's most daring memory project seemed to be the second one regarding childhood pathways through Oshkosh. Susan claimed to like "everything" about what she's seen on Main Street and pronounced that she would draw all of the buildings. Using her typical dot and line drawing style, Susan made what I viewed as her first architectural drawing in class (she usually turns most

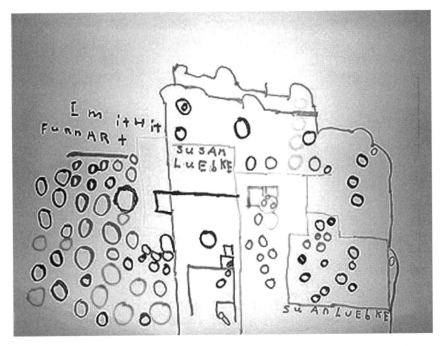

Figure 4.2 Susan's drawing of Main street.

assignments into floral designs). She claimed that the many dots she added after drawing the Main Street buildings were doorknobs, possibly because she recalled visiting many of these businesses.

Sandy

Sixty-year-old Sandy recently joined Project A.R.T., and in my opinion, brought to class an extremely jocular presence. Sandy was also willing and able to talk about the past, although she was definitely ensconced in the present. She loved her own and newly remodeled house and she enjoyed cooking and soap operas, because her mother was the best cook in the world, and "she never gets sick of watching people get married." She went out a few nights a week with friends and discussed her amusing adventures and misadventures as if a teenager. She was also frank, self-confident, and free-spirited in her exchanges. Almost every student that had recently written about working with Sandy mentioned her tendency to exclaim, "How cool are we?" which was then usually followed by a high-five and lots of laughter.

Artistically, Sandy has been forever encouraged by her family to complete velvet poster designs with the latest in designer markers, which seem the most significant factor of her labors. When she came to Project A.R.T., she told us that she was not used to coloring without lines but that she'll quickly get good at it. Sandy's memory is also sharp and sensory. She remembered the smell of her father's job at a steel mill and what a certain storm looked like in 1972 on the way home from a hotel where her mother worked. She enjoyed petting and talking to her two cats who kept her company. A quote from a student journal identified her insightfulness during the first memory project:

> I was trying to get Sandy to think about her favorite toy today and instantly she thought of the Barbie doll, which we then tried to make from model magic. But the funny thing about making the Barbie was that for Sandy it was technically difficult to make it skinny, and then, Sandy decided that Barbies shouldn't be skinny anyhow. She went off about how few people are skinny like that and if you have enough food to eat you should eat it. The more she wondered aloud about this subject the more she made good and strong statements such as, "If I get fat once in a while and my friends don't like it, they can just go on without me—they won't have as much fun." What a cool attitude!

Figure 4.3 Sandy's Barbie rendidtion atop her drawn background.

Joyce

Joyce turned 66 the week I visited her home, and she was excited to show me all of her presents. Generally Joyce's artistic tendencies revolved around pleasant house scenes with images that seemed to be coached. (Joyce formulaically drew trees, houses, flowers, criss-cross windows, etc.) I was not surprised to learn that she did have some art classes in school where the regular education teacher modeled step-by-step rendering toward recognizable symbols. Furthermore, Joyce's process seemed one of orderly habit as she kept her markers in rainbow order, and was concerned with loose marker tops and the correct spelling of words she wished to write. Nonetheless Joyce fulfilled one of the memory projects in her own significant way.

In drawing a map of her favorite place to walk to from her childhood home, Joyce began gathering pink colored markers and copied the word *Primrose* from

one of them. Then she added above this the directions *find the . . . .* After this, she composed the drawing into a bunch of rosebuds. It all seemed like an inexplicable playful diversion from the subject until her partner was able to ask the right questions and determine that Joyce had once lived on a Rosetree Street or Avenue and was impressed by the many flowers along this route. A university student commented, "I thought most artists were going to focus on drawing their favorite place to go but Joyce seemed to like the walk itself."

Figure 4.4 Joyce's primrose drawing.

Mike

True to demographics, we had more older women in Project A.R.T. than men. But Mike, who had recently become a senior citizen, disavows much of what the men of our class like, such as, the Packers, politics, and television/movies. He was a mellow man, transformed from his early days of being a coarse truck driver. Mike was cognitively disabled due to a traumatic brain injury as the result of a trucking accident in which he swerved to avoid hitting a child. He was blind and suffered memory loss since his twenties and thirties. Additionally, Mike had lost many family members tragically as well as a girlfriend last year. If anyone exuded a paradigm of loving life and mulling over death, it was Mike. Almost like a minister, he expressed disgust for a world that ignored the meek, the homeless, and so on. But although his jargon could be tough and sarcastic, Mike was a truly kind and gentle human being, the type that would recall a teddy bear as his favorite childhood toy. He exuded, perhaps, the "integrative understanding" many scholars such as Heta Kauppinen (1987) discussed as the ability to transcend the tension between conflicting opposites. He planned each art project as a gift—usually for a residential employee or other acquaintance. The memory projects were poignant for Mike because he visited a past he often kept to himself.

The third of the three projects seemed to be the most challenging for Mike. Mike's recall about the best place in Oshkosh was immediately his favorite Friday night fish fry restaurant. He then added that the most beautiful place in Oshkosh was the Old Lutheran Church that needed repair with a "fancy old" altar that made him feel peaceful. Mike stopped attending church because he couldn't follow the pace of services, but he agreed to draw how he remembered church despite the fact that he disliked drawing because of his vision impair-

Figure 4.5 Mike's drawing of a church interior.

54

ment. For Mike, since he attended this church in childhood, this was a reference with his distant past that he rarely acknowledged.

A relevant student journal from that night with Mike read,

> Mike (even though he dresses conservatively and talks straightforward) seems like more of a hippie than a lot of young people trying to be like that today. He is against war, he thinks there should be more welfare and he told me that if he won the lottery he'd give it all away to a homeless shelter. He's totally unselfish, and even with the church drawing, he thought he should give it to a city council member so they'd fix it up.

Implications for ART Education

It is difficult to measure the worth of this study beyond my observations, the student journal responses, the apparent satisfaction of the Project A.R.T. students at the end of classes, and evidence of creative departures in their artwork. Like any relationship with art or people, time will tell its full impact on our learning and growth. However, after four years of watching the Project A.R.T. class transform, I can honestly say that the most rewarding and substantial activities were those that encouraged a dialog between the senior student and their young university assistant, and then, between student and their artwork. The more diverse the pairs in terms of age or disposition, the greater each party seemed affected by interacting with one another. And the more engaged the participants, their work was richer and more creative. Jean Gasen Romaniuk (1976) questioned the ability to train creativity in the older adults via participation in arts workshops as part of her graduate thesis. I would extend this question to the guidance of seniors with cognitive disabilities for whom art making is often trained and made routine at the expense of challenge or psychological exploration. I believe projects that call for autobiographical input (bolstered by the support and recording of avidly listening assistants) have led to new ventures for us in Project A.R.T. For most people who have had minimal art opportunities or training, materializing an image from one's memory is baffling because a disconnection arises when perceived technical drawing deficiencies interrupt the process of visual description. But when young university assistants encouraged mental meandering and memory recall/interpretation from the older adult artists they seemed more able to sustain or even conjure details of past images. This in itself does not imply creativity but it provides a certain basis of confidence from which creative decision making more easily flows.

While many Project A.R.T. seniors veered toward making *functional* art, I believe the memory project also validated the value of art for reflection's sake and the ensuing *new looks* to their creations were exclaimed by guardians and caregivers, who were oblivious to the project's intent. These genuine commendations often heartened Project A.R.T. students to try and repeat the essences of such success.

Finally, focusing on youthful experiences unites cognitively disabled older adults and university students, because for both these groups, childhood is in the past and often amusing. It is also a looking glass into poignant moments that have shaped all of our self-awareness. Artistic interpretation of such sentiments is invaluable.

References

Alexenberg, M. (2000). *Intergenerational collaboration in pubic art.* Los Angeles: Paper presented at the National Art Education Association Conference.

Bliss, J., & Perlstein, S. (1994). *Generating community: Intergenerational partnerships through the expressive arts.* New York: Elders Share the Arts.

Gardner, H. (1990). *Art education and human development.* Los Angeles: The Getty Center.

Hendricks, J. (1995). *Meaning of reminiscence and life review.* New York: Baywood Book Co.

Hoffman, D. H. (1992). *Arts for older adults: An enhancement of life.* Englewood Cliffs, NJ: Prentice Hall.

Kauppinen, H. (1987). Aging: Aging as a theme in art and education. *Art Education, 40*(4), 42-51.

Kauppinen, H. (1990). Changing perspectives on older adults' mental abilities and educational needs: Implications for art education. *Studies in Art Education, 31*(2), 99-105.

Rentsch, T. (1997). Aging as becoming oneself: A philosophical ethics of late life. *Journal of Aging Studies, 4*(11), 263-271.

Romaniuk, J. G. (1978) Training creativity in the elderly: an examination of attitudes, self-perception and ability. Madison, WI.: University of Wisconsin. Master's Thesis.

Rubinstein, R. (1987). The significance of personal objects to older people. *Journal of Aging Studies, 3*(1), 225-238.

Tingey, C. (1988). *Down's Syndrome: A resource handbook.* Boston: Little and Brown.

5

Michelle Tony Zelkowitz

Bringing The Outdoors In: An Intergenerational Community Service Mural Art Project

Overview

In a small rural city, population 20,000, in the northern tier of New York State from October 2000—June 2001, a high school art teacher (the researcher) developed and administered an intergenerational art program, funded by a grant from the local teacher resource center. Participants included the art teacher, 21 high school students, a campus minister and a principal from a private northeastern Catholic high school, and 80 residents, an administrator, and two physical therapy staff from a county nursing home.

The art teacher recruited students from the campus ministry and her art class for the program. The adolescent volunteers, under the art teacher's supervision, visited residents two times a week after school for one to two hours. Nursing

57

Figure: 5.1

Painting by Adrianne Longino.

home staff introduced the adolescents to the residents to establish relationships by engaging in recreational activities, i.e., checkers, chess, bingo and word games. Adolescents took photographs of the residents that were used as resources for painting a mural together on the physical therapy room wall.

After several discussions about the mural content with the administrator, staff, residents, and students, the art teacher recommended an outdoor theme for the wall mural. Students invited staff and residents to suggest scenes reflecting the changing seasons of the rural Adirondack landscape. Everyone collected images from magazines and calendars to help with planning the design of the mural. Some students also used their own photographs of the Adirondack landscape. Then, on a cold winter afternoon, staff, students, residents, the art teacher, and the campus minister met in the dining area of the nursing home to create a design. Students laid out resource images on two large tables. After much discussion, a few students detailed four scenes using selected elements from the resource images. One student recorded the suggestions, and four adolescents volunteered to create one pencil sketch for each season. Finally, at another meeting in the physical therapy room, students, the administrator, staff and the art teacher agreed to use the sketches for summer and fall to begin painting the mural. Over a six-month period, students, staff, and residents added details to the painting.

Figure: 5.2

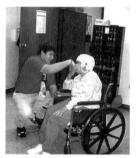

Figure: 5.3

Residents, many of whom were confined to wheelchairs, usually watched the adolescents paint. However, on three occasions, with encouragement and assistance from the staff and adolescents, several residents also painted on the wall mural. The students paired with residents and painted side-by-side to complete the background scene. A few students also volunteered to sketch some of the residents for use in the mural. One sketch used for the mural included a resident in a wheelchair pushed by a female adolescent. Another drawing of the resident cat was also used.

58

Upon the completion of the 8-foot by 22-foot mural, an unveiling ceremony honored all of the participants. Local dignitaries, family members, residents, and students attended the event. A videotaped broadcast of the event appeared on the evening news, as well as a story and photograph on the front page of the local newspaper.

Purpose of Study

This study examines how participation in an intergenerational community service art project, creating a wall mural in a nursing home, might affect the personal development of adolescents. Two primary questions guided the research: How might adolescent student artists' involvement in the design and painting of a mural with residents in a nursing home affect their personal development? How might adolescents' participation in voluntary community service help them develop into caring, community-minded adults?

Research Methods

Ethnographic and phenomenological qualitative research techniques and art-based research techniques were used to gather participants' perceptions of the program. On site, the researcher made participant observations, the primary method of ethnographers (Patton, 1990), and recorded the daily interactions of the participants. According to Kuehne and Collins (1997) "Observational research, though not without its shortcomings, should be widely used to study and evaluate intergenerational program effectiveness and the relationships among people within these programs" (p. 183). In keeping with phenomenological research methods, the researcher also conducted in-depth 30-45 minute interviews (Leedy & Ormond, 2001) of ten adolescent participants and two physical therapy staff members using standardized open and close-ended questions. The use of artistic inquiry methods, such as photography, creative writing, and aesthetic critiques, were also employed to gather, analyze, and present data, and for engagement in the creative process (Hervey, 2000).

The small sample of individuals who volunteered to be interviewed upon completion of the project were two 9th grade males, one 10th grade female, five 11th grade females, one 12th grade male, one 12th grade female, and two female physical therapy staff. Most of the adolescent interviewees were in campus ministry and/or art class and participated fully in the program, visiting residents, photographing residents, and painting on the wall mural. Four adolescent interviewees also created sketches for the mural. Over 50 percent of the adolescent interviewees were White, female, 11th graders.

The researcher/art teacher and the adolescent participants used digital photography to initiate relationships with the residents, record observations, document

Figure: 5.4

visits, and engage in the creative mural activity with residents. Photographs documented the development of the intergenerational relationships and the process of painting the mural and provided source material for the content of the painting. Upon the completion of the mural, photographs were also used to create multimedia presentations that were shown to local officials and art educators.

During the program, the researcher collaborated with three of the adolescent participants to construct an instrument to interview participants. The following questions guided the process: How did participating in the program affect the lives of the adolescents and residents? How did the adolescents' experiences in the nursing home affect the design of the mural? How did the nursing home staff and the residents influence the painting of the wall mural? How did the mural change the nursing home environment?

Instruments developed by the researcher were based on the work of Hamburg, (1997), Lerner and Galambos (1998), Youniss, et al. (1999), Eccles and Barber (1999), Quatman and Swanson (2002), Larson (2000), Delle Fave and Bassi (2000), Beamon (2001), and Bridges, et al. (2001). Four indicators of personal development in

Figure: 5.5

adolescence were studied: social development; emotional growth; work ethics; and physical, mental, and emotional well-being.

Figure: 5.6

Interview questions were both structured and unstructured, consisting of fixed response and open-ended questions, as well as follow-up questions, based on the individual's responses. Questions in the adolescent questionnaire were piloted with three adolescents. As a result, participants suggested new questions and some were modified. The researcher/art teacher recorded, videotaped, and transcribed each interview.

Responses, collected from multiple-choice questions, were converted to percentages and displayed in bar graphs, which were used to examine and compare adolescents' and physical therapy staff's responses. Similar replies to open-ended questions were highlighted to see if a pattern of responses occurred. Photographs and journal entries were reviewed to evaluate the type and number of activities the adolescents engaged in, and to investigate which activities may have most affected the outcome of the study.

Data collected by the researcher through observations and self-reporting may reflect the bias of the researcher and the participants. Therefore, it would be unwise to generalize about adolescents' involvement in an intergenerational community service art project based solely on this study.

Findings

The most significant finding was that intergenerational relationships formed as a result of participation in the program. In interviews, adolescents indicated that they formed close relationships with the residents. Some comments follow:

> "Most of them were very welcoming and accepting and looked forward to seeing us. . . . There were a lot of people that I became surprisingly close to."

> "I got to know a few of them pretty well."

> "I got close to one particular resident and we have a pretty good relationship."

> "Throughout the time that I visited . . . I got to be close to some of the [residents] there."

Most adolescent interviewees perceived their intergenerational experiences positively. *Figure 5.7* shows adolescents' perceptions of six intergenerational experiences: (a) visiting with residents, (b) visiting with residents and other students, (c) posing with residents for pictures, (d) taking pictures of residents, (e) painting with residents, and (f) painting while residents watched. The participants were asked to respond if their experiences were "very positive," "positive," "negative," "very negative," or "I don't know."

Two adolescents (20 percent) thought that taking pictures with residents and painting with residents were negative experiences. However, as seen in *Figure 5.8,* the two staff members interviewed believed 100 percent of the experiences between the adolescents and the residents were positive. (In *Figure 5.7 & 5.8*

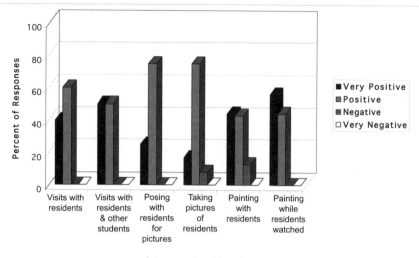

Figure: 5.7

numbers were rounded off to the nearest whole percent and did not include the response, "I don't know.")

Figure 5.9 illustrates adolescents' perceptions of how their experiences at the nursing home advanced their personal development in the four-targeted areas: social development; emotional growth; work ethics; and physical, mental, and emotional well-being. Adolescents reflected on their experiences and responded,

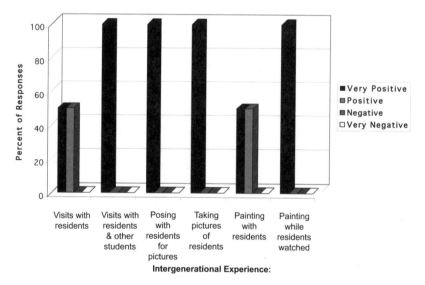

Figure: 5.8

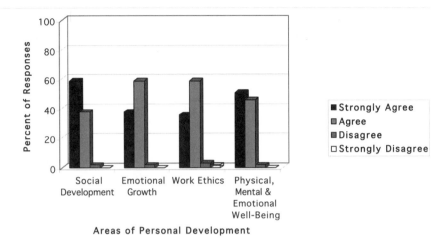

Figure: 5.9

"strongly agree," "agree," "disagree," or "strongly disagree" to 40 statements of attributes, which lead to improved personal development. For example, adolescents indicated that they learned how to communicate more effectively, to work cooperatively with others, to control their emotions, to express themselves appropriately, to show empathy, optimism, and humor. The adolescents also believed that they became more aware of their own strengths, including the ability to plan and set goals, to problem solve, and to resolve conflicts thoughtfully and in a reflective manner.

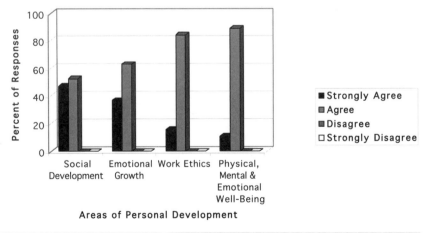

Figure: 5.10

Generally, adolescents' responses indicated advances in the four-targeted areas of personal development. Three adolescents (30 percent) disagreed with some of the statements in one or more of the targeted areas of personal development. However, as shown in *Figure 5.10*, the staff believed that the adolescents improved in all the targeted areas of personal development.

Observations (photographs and journal entries) and responses to interview questions revealed adolescents, who consistently visited with the residents at the nursing home, developed not only relationships with the residents, but also a heightened feeling of self-awareness. One staff member noted, "I was very pleasantly surprised . . . I have to be honest . . . I saw some great relationships form . . . between some of the residents and the students. They did not seem intimidated at all, as I would have expected."

The adolescents also changed their attitudes about aging and older people, and behaved differently, after frequent intergenerational interactions. For example, at the beginning of the program, a male participant said, "I wasn't sure what it was going to be like [volunteering at the nursing home] . . . I was a little nervous about doing it at first. I thought . . . with the age difference, with the generation difference . . . it would be too much to overcome." Within a few weeks, his attitude about aging and older people changed:

> There's so much stuff that you can learn from . . . [older] people that people are neglecting to research and find out. It's . . . first hand accounts. . . .They were there. And you can't really write everything you experience firsthand down in textbooks. So it's a way of experiencing history. . . . I like history a lot, so it's beneficial.

The researcher also observed changes in his behavior. The adolescent smiled and maintained close physical contact with several residents and engaged in many activities: conversations, games of chess and checkers, poses for pictures, and the transport of residents to and from the physical therapy room.

A female adolescent had similar experiences and offered this advice to other students interested in volunteering at the nursing home:

> It may be intimidating or frightening at first, but once you get to know [the residents] and deal with them, it's not really . . . frightening; it's nice. To have somebody want to see you . . . and [to see] their faces lighten up and brighten up when they see you, because you are really an integral part of their stay at the nursing home. . . . It was definitely a new experience and . . . fun.

Discussion

The findings of this study raise several issues that deserve further attention. Are compassion and/or empathy for older people of value to adolescents as they move into adulthood? Does participation in an intergenerational art project lead adolescents to a more meaningful and productive adult life and encourage them to connect more with their community? Would older adults have the benefits of a prolonged life and/or better health as a result of social contact with adolescents?

Figure: 5.11

Studies have documented the therapeutic value of intergenerational activities (Clark, 1991; Weston, Owen, McGuire, Backman & Allen, 1993) and "show that adults can materially contribute to the healthy development of adolescents outside their own families, and in so doing, also contribute to enhanced community trust and connections" (Scales, 2001, p. 69).

Adolescents, involved in adult-supported activities that provide opportunities to practice skills (Delle Fave & Bassi, 2000), build an identity (Erickson, 1968; Waterman, 1984; Harter, 1990; Nurmi, Poole, & Kalakoski, 1997; Marcia, 2002; Meeus, Silbereisen, Nurmi, Zimmermann, & Becker-Stoll, 2002), and become socially responsible within the culture (Jarvinen & Nicholls, 1996; Catalano, Berglund, Ryan, Lonczak, & Hawkins, 1999) advance in their personal development. Intergenerational community service art projects provide adolescents "with nourishing, growth-enhancing opportunities" (Roeser, Eccles, & Sameroff, 2000, p. 443) that help them develop positive attributes and contribute to society.

Developing more intergenerational art programs and evaluating their effectiveness is worthy of our continued attention. As more programs emerge, researchers will be able to more fully examine the challenges and understand and exploit the benefits associated with building relationships between adolescents and older adults. Longitudinal studies with both qualitative and quantitative methods will reveal the

Figure: 5.12

long-term effects of intergenerational programming. These studies will contribute to our understanding of the needs of adolescents and older people and may help to establish high quality intergenerational partnerships. As these programs evolve, policies might be put into effect to make positive changes in the way we communicate between generations and care for one another.

> Today, with the greying of America and with diminishing economic resources for the social and educational needs of both young and old, intergenerational creative arts programs have proven to be an inspiring and effective way to build community. In trying to develop mutual understanding, and community connections, these programs have become an important vehicle for linking generations and cultures. (Perlstein, 1996)

In the sheltered environment of the nursing home's caring adult community, the adolescents developed more self-confidence and improved interpersonal skills, and thereby became more responsible individuals. In the words of the adolescent participants:

Figure: 5.13

Taking part in such an experience led us to share our own stories and memories. Some friendships began, while others developed, respect was gained and given, laughs were shared and smiles filled the room.

The mural project was "challenging," "empowering," "eye-opening," "enlightening," "inspiring," "fun," "history-bridging," and " a cooperative-effort."

I'd recommend that [adolescents] get involved because it teaches you . . . team spirit . . . [how to] cooperate with others [and] respect for the [older people].

The mural project taught us more about life and giving of ourselves than any classroom experience. All the hard work, long hours, and exhausting expectations were worth every second.

This mural as a whole, combined not only our artistic and creative talents, but growth in our minds and our hearts. I don't believe that any of us can walk away from this experience untouched, and I can only hope that some of what we have learned shines through the effort that we put into the mural itself. . . . Anyone that has an opportunity like this should feel incredibly lucky and they should know that they [would] be forever changed.

Hopefully, the adolescents will continue their commitment to volunteer in their communities. May this research inform practitioners of the benefits of engaging adolescents in art activities with older people and motivate them to action.

References

Beamon, G. W. (2001). *Teaching with the adolescent in mind.* Arlington Heights, IL: Skylight Professional Development.

Bridges, L. J., Margie, N. G., & Zaff, J. F. (2001). *Background for community-level work on emotional well-being in adolescence: Reviewing the literature on contributing factors.* Washington, DC: Child Trends, Inc.

Catalano, R., Berglund, M., Ryan, J., Lonczak, H., & Hawkins, D. (1999). *Positive youth development in the United States: Research findings on evaluations of positive youth development programs.* Seattle, WA: United States Department of Health and Human Services.

Clark, P. (1991). *Intergenerational arts in the nursing home: A handbook.* Westport, CT: Greenwood Press.

Delle Fave, A., & Bassi, M. (2000). The quality of experience in adolescents' daily lives: Developmental perspectives. *Genetic, Social, and General Psychology Monographs, 126*(3), 347-368.

Eccles, J. S., & Barber, B. L. (1999). Student council, volunteering, basketball, or marching band: What kind of extracurricular matters? *Journal of Adolescent Research, 14*(1), 10-43.

Erickson, E. H. (1968). *Identity, youth, and crisis.* New York: W.W. Norton and Company.

Hamburg, D. V. (1997). Toward a strategy for healthy adolescent development. *American Journal of Psychiatry, 154*(6, Supplement), 7-12.

Harter, S. (1990). Self and identity development. In S. Feldman & G. Elliott (Eds.), *At the threshold: The developing adolescent* (pp. 352-387). Cambridge, MA: Harvard University Press.

Hervey, L. W. (2000). *Artistic inquiry in dance/movement therapy: Creative alternatives for research.* Springfield, IL: Charles C. Thomas.

Jarvinen, D. W., & Nicholls, J. G. (1996). Adolescents' social goals, beliefs about the causes of social success, and satisfaction in peer relations. *Developmental Psychology, 32*(3), 435-441.

Kuehne, V. S., & Collins, C. L. (1997). Observational research in intergenerational programming: Need and opportunity. *Journal of Gerontological Social Work, 28*(1/2), 183-193.

Larson, R. W. (2000). Toward a psychology of positive youth development. *American Psychologist, 55*(1), 170-183.

Leedy, P. D., & Ormrod, J. E. (2001). *Practical research: Planning and design.* (7th ed.). Upper Saddle River, NJ: Prentice Hall, Inc.

Lerner, R. M., & Galambos, N. L. (1998). Adolescent development: Challenges and opportunities for research, programs, and policies. *Annual Review of Psychology, 49*, 413-447.

Marcia, J. (2002). Adolescence, identity, and the Bernardone family. *Identity, 2*(3), 199-209.

Meeus, W., Silbereisen, R., Nurmi, J.E., Zimmermann, P., & Becker-Stoll, F. (2002). Stability of attachment representations during adolescence: The influence of ego-identity status. *Journal of Adolescence, 25*(1), 107-124.

Nurmi, J.E., Poole, M., & Kalakoski, V. (1997). Age differences in adolescent identity exploration and commitment in urban and rural environments. *Journal of Adolescence, 19*(5), 443-453.

Patton, M. Q. (1990). *Qualitative evaluation and research methods*. (2nd ed.). Newbury Park, CA: Sage Publications, Inc.

Perlstein, S. (1996). *Arts Programs Uniting Generations*. In A. Sherman (Ed). The Arts and Older Americans: Monographs: November 1996, Volume 5, Number 8 (p 5). Retrieved August 10, 2004 from http://pubs.artusa.org/library/ARTS033/html/5.html

Quatman, T., & Swanson, C. (2002). Academic self-disclosure in adolescence. *Genetic, Social, and General Psychology Monographs, 128*(1), 47-75.

Roeser, R. W., Eccles, J. S., & Sameroff, A. J. (May 2000). School as a context of early Adolescents' academic and social-emotional development: A summary of research findings. *The Elementary School Journal, 100*(5), 443-473.

Scales, P. C. (2001). The public image of adolescents. *Society, 38*(4), 64-70.

Waterman, A. (1984). Identity formation: Discovery or creation? *Journal of Early Adolescence, 4*(4), 329-341.

Weston, R., Owen, M., McGuire, F., Backman, K., & Allen, J. (1993). The intergenerational entrepreneurship demonstration project: An innovative approach to intergenerational mentoring. *The Journal of Physical Education, Recreation & Dance, 64*(8), 48-51.

Youniss, J., McLellan, J. A., & Yates, Y. (1999). The role of community service in identity development: Normative, unconventional, and deviant orientations. *Journal of Adolescent Research, 14*(2), 248-261.

6

Steve Willis

The Acoma Experience

Overview

This chapter discusses the benefits of dissolving traditional (Western) classroom walls to allow for direct cultural experiences in Native Americana by non-Natives. Specifically, a view of how selected art teachers from Missouri experienced traditional Acoma pottery first-hand through instruction from potter Daisy Aragon, an Acoma Tribal Clan Grandmother.

Through direct, and sometimes subtle, interpersonal exchanges the art teachers experienced Southwest Native American Pottery in personal ways not found in photography, video, or text, which directly influenced the curricula developed by the participants. A first-person dialog of the art teachers' cultural experiences is presented in relationship to their curricular development and implementation of

Figure: 6.1. Acoma Pottery: View of the many samples of traditional Acoma pottery made by the residents of Sky City.

these experiences for their students in each respective school and art program. The range of discussions includes making pottery tools such as the yucca brush, construction of the dung kiln, and the food and environment of the Acoma Reservation. Connections are proposed as to the feasibility of this experience being translatable to a wide array of important educational experiences from cultural enclaves down the street or across the country. (The titles of Grandma, Aunt, Uncle, Brother, Sister, and Cousin are respectful among Native Americans.)

The Acoma Experience

Seven non-Native American art education graduate students from Southwest Missouri State University [SMSU] left Springfield, Missouri in June of 2003 to discover how the Acoma People live and how master potter, Grandma Daisy Aragon, makes traditional pottery, builds a traditional dung kiln, bakes horno bread, and lives the traditional Acoma life of a clan Grandmother. What these seven discovered was much richer than simply a visit to a potter's studio. They experienced a friendly and wise Grandmother who was open with her home, culture, and stories. They discovered traditional teaching from generation to generation that is embedded into most traditional Native American cultures. Their interactions with Grandma Daisy, her sons Fred and Joe Aragon, her grandsons Eyo and Wayne, and her sister, Aunt Pearl Valdo, etched durable memories.

Introduction to the Acoma Reservation

Interstate 40 cuts a thin line through the Acoma Reservation in western New Mexico. Closer to Gallup than Albuquerque, the arid region is filled with sagebrush, yucca cactus, and pinion. Buttes and canyons fill the visual expanse and ancient memories of mountains and volcanic eruptions are still found in the old stories. The reverence of the earth is obvious with the traditional Acoma People. They carefully maintain a site known in English as Sky City, which according to anthropologists, has been occupied since 1150 C.E. (common era) and is the longest continually inhabited location in the United States (see http://www.puebloofacoma.org/). The word Acoma comes from, "Ako: to be ready, to have everything one needs" (Daisy Aragon, personal notes, Summer, 2003).

Sky City is a common stop for tourists traveling on Interstate 40. There is a convenient visitors' center operated by the Acoma Nation that allows non-

Figure: 6.2. View of Sky City architecture and Kiva ladders (A Kiva is a ceremonial structure.) Much of the original architecture exists today. Photo-graph by the author.

Acoma to visit Sky City, which sits on top of a butte high above Coyote Canyon. As one drives south from the interstate and around through the Acoma Nation, it is easy to imagine how the Spanish army of Francisco Vaques de Coronado in 1540 would have seen a similar vista, thought to be the first White man to encounter the Acoma People.

After the Pueblo Revolts and Acoma was nearly destroyed by Governor Juan de Oñate in 1598, peace was restored and the San Esteban del Rey Mission was built. The Acoma men, who carried the beams on their backs from Mt. Taylor, built the mission. In accordance to spiritual beliefs, the beams were not allowed to touch the ground on the approximately 35-mile journey, and were then hauled up the nearly vertical 367 foot incline (Willis, 2003).

I first visited the wide, magical vista of Coyote Canyon over 20 years ago. Each time I go back, either alone or with students, there is an exaltation of beauty as clean as the sage-filled air. It has become a special place for me, a non-Acoma, who understands only a small amount of the rich and diverse Acoma culture, which is bound by ancient rituals and ceremonies. The Acoma Nation is a thriving culture, rich in traditional history and living in the 21st century with vigor. This is a culture of traditional customs that considers changes brought in by outside influences. A tribally owned casino brings financial stability and a growing infrastructure of tribal facilities for the Acoma People. It has been my experience that the Acoma People are exceptionally friendly and willing to share much of their history and culture. It is because of these extraordinary experiences that I do not hesitate to take students to the Acoma Reservation for their own experiences of hiking through the arid terrain, making traditional pottery, collecting dung for a traditional kiln, baking horno bread, and listening to the stories of the Elders. These are the things that cannot be found in books or videos, or by merely visiting Sky City. This understanding must be lived to plant the seed of experience that blooms as a tree of awareness; an awareness of otherness and difference that converge as adjacent lives into humanity.

The seven SMSU (Southern Missouri State University) graduate students worked with master potter, Grandma Daisy Aragon and her sister, Aunt Pearl Valdo, and collected their own experiences to plant in their own classrooms. Those seeds of intergenerational and intracultural learning and teaching were fertile and have blossomed into a not previously understood awareness. The Elders planted lessons formulated by these teachers for their students far removed from pueblo life. Teaching from one generation to the next is a traditional Native experience. What Grandma Daisy learned from her mother, she shares with others. Her sharing is not limited by culture or language—she is fluent in English as well as Acoma. This accumulated knowledge lives within one generation but is shared among other generations and cultures.

Participants

The art teachers were: Sherrie Copenhaver (Parkview High School, Springfield, MO), Jennifer Czyzewski (South Calloway R-11, Mokane, MO), Jamie Gassel (New Covenant Academy, Springfield, MO), Allison Harris (Harrison Junior High School, Harrison, AR), Evert Wayne Henry (Lebanon Junior High School, Lebanon, MO), Stephanie Rieser (Parkview High School, Springfield, MO) and Cheryl Sloan (Stockton R-1 School, Stockton, MO). Each narrates the experience differently and brought home to their respective classrooms a curriculum based on a wealth of personal experiences that are durable and translatable.

Figure: 6.3. Acoma Oven: View of a Sky City horno bread oven, which is close to the water cistern (currently used for livestock) and the single tree (cottonwood). Photograph by the author.

Preparation of Non-Natives for Imersion into the Acoma Culture

Many non-natives have an acculturated understanding of what an "Indian" is. Partially, this comes from books, but mostly comes from Hollywood and sports. Non-Natives hear war chants, see Styrofoam tomahawks, and dyed chicken feathers at sporting events, and according to Delacruz (2003), have become numb to the covert racism. Deloria (1992) points out that Native Americans are much different than normally understood by non-Natives. Native American cultures, like others, are complex in understanding and wealthy in nuance. The students who visited the Acoma Reservation had multiple readings, but *The Indians of the American Imagination*, chapter two in *God is Red* (Deloria, 1992),

Racism American Style and Resistance to Change: Art Education's Role in the Indian Mascot Issue (Delacruz, 2003), and *Wheel of Misfortune* (Barlett & Steele, 2002) generated the most interesting discussions.

Research

This group of teachers was directed to develop curricular methodologies in relationship to first-hand experiences gained on the Acoma Reservation. Course expectations placed an emphasis on developing teaching strategies addressing studio processes that reflect Native American aesthetical, critical, historical, and cultural components. Specifically, students were asked to investigate social, historical, pedagogical, philosophical, and evaluative topics germane to their personal teaching practices within Southwest Native American cultural contextualization. The two questions motivating this research were: "How do non-Natives respond to Reservation experiences?" and "How will these experiences affect their pedagogy and curriculum?" The following are brief excerpts from their experiences on the Reservation, their responses to the readings, and their curriculum units.

Participants' Perceptions

Harris thought that much of the racist issues discussed by Delacruz were cultural differences and misunderstandings and concluded that,

> "Though I am part of this White culture, I am female and understand a little of the turmoil and the desire to be taken seriously as a person, and not a symbol of something I am not, nor do I want to be. In my opinion, the same can be true of the American Indians who do not seem to be taken seriously because of the misconceptions brought forth by the early White man, and those that still continue today."

Henry had a different reaction to racism, and

> In reading the article by Delacruz, I found myself becoming more sensitive to the issue of racism against Native Americans. I had not given much thought to the stereotype mascots that sports teams portray. I did not have much of an opinion either way. After reading the article, I have gained an awareness of the social issue of racism in mascots. While out shopping this week [prior to the trip], I noticed several items that could be considered offensive. I also began to see the reactions of those I talked with when I mentioned my plans for the summer. Several people made jokes about me not getting scalped, wasting my money away at the casino, or bringing back an Indian squaw. Although they were only joking, I noticed how strongly the stereotypes are embedded in our [White] culture.

Responding to *God is Red*, Rieser wrote, "How could we be so ignorant, so unsympathetic? Could it be that we became desensitized by all of those Hollywood images? I was." Coppenhaver thought that "the exploitation by non-Indians in regard to tribal religions, celebrations, and customs was disgusting, but also predictable." Czyzewski responded:

> Non-natives cannot truly understand or relate to Native religions because they lack the fundamental ingredient: being a Native person, having been raised and nurtured in a Native experience. While I believe non-natives have the right to research and study religions of all types, adopting another culture's religion is a far more threatening move. White Americans must improve their understanding of Native cultures in order to realize that what is theirs culturally does not automatically include or belong to whites as well.

Sloan replied candidly to *Wheel of Misfortune*:

> I am opposed to gambling. I feel there is a side of humans that when stimulated brings out the worst. There is an old saying, "two wrongs don't make a right." It's hard to look at gambling and see the benefits. But on the other hand it is hard to look at families in need, communities lacking proper schools, a police force, and fire protection. It appears that the "need" is greater than the moral issue of gambling. Ideally if the profits of the casinos were to go to the tribes and all its needs, I could set my negative feelings aside.

These conversations were common topics among the group. The teachers returned home with a much different understanding, as diverse as each person's story. Some liked the Fourth of July conversation with Joe Aragon more than baking horno bread, while others preferred the personal histories of Grandma Daisy more than making traditional pottery and constructing the kiln for the dung firing.

The Art Teachers' Experiences

Sherrie Copenhaver found the trip memorable and thought every experience carried its own meaning from pottery to food to conversations. Returning to her school, she found it important that her Art Foundations students:

> investigate the artwork and how it reflected the history of the Pueblo people and culture; understand how earlier works might have influenced contemporary artwork, and how current world events might influence artworks of the future; recognize symbols and imagery that were common to Pueblo art;

and, identify some conditions used to determine whether objects from the Southwestern Pueblo culture can be considered art.

Her discussion of cultural value of art forms may be found in a similar way in her response to Hucko (1999), as she stated:

> In the opening paragraph of the book, the author stated that pottery was "First produced out of necessity to hold water, cook, and store grain, (yet) it has evolved into a refined and coveted art form," I love this statement. (Copenhaver, course work, 2003)

Jennifer Czyzewski planned multiple activities to share with her middle school students. She wanted students to: (a) gain an understanding of the history of the Acoma culture through a group study of artifacts, a discussion of these artifacts, and a report on the significance of this society and its influences on our own; (b) create a traditional Acoma seed pot by using their [Acoma] techniques: pinching, smoothing and burnishing; (c) construct a yucca paintbrush to use in creating a page of Acoma designs; (d) understand the traditional pottery firing process of a dung pit kiln; and (e) participate in a class critique in order to build a thorough understanding of how their own work fits into the multicultural aesthetic of the culture studied in this unit.

Jamie Gassel reports that,

> The trip to New Mexico was a tremendous learning experience for me, both as a student and a teacher. I had the opportunity to see firsthand how the Acoma People live. I visited the ancient Sky City as well as modern homes. I felt their native land more than I saw it. (personal notes, Gassel, 2003)

She also noticed that the Acoma people have a great tradition of using the resources of their surroundings. An example of this is the traditional pottery because the materials all come from their land, including the clay, the pigments, and the yucca brushes.

> Being on the Acoma Reservation was an aesthetic experience for me; one I share with my students. I passed on to my students the techniques used to make the pottery as well as pictures and stories I shared about the hike down from Sky City, the food, and the people. (personal notes, Gassel, winter, 2003.)

Allison Harris felt that she could share her experiences with her students by exposing them to her curriculum unit, the *Southwest Indian Arts: Emphasis on Acoma Pottery and Pueblo Tribes*. According to her, the students will explore the idea of multiculturalism as they compare their own society to the Native

American tribes of the Southwest, pueblo artwork, and traditions. She proposes that through discussions of Southwest Native American culture, students will develop an understanding of life outside their own societies. They will study history, culture, tribal art and traditions that exist today. Students will create artwork using traditional Acoma pottery techniques and natural tools. (Harris, 2003, course curriculum)

In this plan for her eighth-graders, Harris will discuss the cultural background of the Acoma People so that the students will be able to distinguish differences between the old and new ways of reservation life as well as the differences and similarities between Native Americans of today and their Euro-American contemporaries. To accomplish this, she will have students (a) explore traditional symbols used in Acoma pottery and how they relate to the surrounding area; (b) familiarize students with the hand-building technique used by Acoma potters (the work transitioning from daily use to an art form); (c) have the students experience the use of natural materials in making of Acoma style pottery, such as the Yucca brush; (d) explore the process of firing clay using natural materials like dung used by traditional Acoma potters; and (e) complete the unit by reviewing cultural facts and ideas so that students have both a product and a comprehensive understanding of the Acoma People and Acoma pottery.

Wayne Henry feels that his students are living in a quickly changing multicultural world and yet have little chance to personally experience various cultures. His ideas of his students' making pottery using methods learned through his direct contact with Acoma potters and the discussions of the Acoma People will provide his students with a comprehensive understanding of the Acoma culture and artworks. Students will use information presented from Henry's firsthand experiences and visual resources to create individual works and understand the history related to artworks of Acoma and Pueblo Natives. Henry reports that:

> The students have been very responsive to the creations of the potteries. It is very good for my students to return to a previously learned technique [pinch pot method], refreshing the method in the mind and in the hands. I am using this unit as a review and also a post-test to see the development of student skills since the first of the semester. (Henry, personal notes, winter, 2003)

His objectives are to lead his students to maintain a working artist's journal, create pottery using the methods of the Acoma potters, participate in a dung firing, and write a narrative critique of the process including details of the various steps taken to create the artwork. He plans to relate his personal experiences of traveling to Sky City and the surrounding area, describe the family life, the climate, and the key survival necessities, which will be supported by a

PowerPoint presentation, photographs, posters, and texts. In reflection, he concludes:

> For myself, I would not give up my experience for anything. I have been using the experience as a catalyst to spark my own thoughts and philosophies about my relationship to the clay and the earth forces around me (Henry, personal notes, winter, 2003).

Stephanie Rieser took a different slant to apply her experiences by incorporating it into the study of architecture using three Missouri ShowMe Standards by requiring the students to: (a) discover and evaluate patterns and relationships in information and structures; (b) identify, analyze and compare the institutions, traditions, and art forms of the past and present societies; and (c) exchange information, questions, and ideas while recognizing the perspectives of others. For one example, she noted in her curricula that she expects her students to compare and contrast visually, socially, and culturally the architecture of the Pueblo with that of Western 20th century architecture.

She reflected that by coming from a Midwestern middle class culture, Acoma was an impressive, eye opening experience. Grandma Daisy and Aunt Pearl shared their home, their knowledge of the ancient skill of Acoma pottery, and fed them several times a day. She remembered the July 4th gathering with the Aragon family and their friends where they were treated to wonderful food and thought provoking conversations with Daisy's son, Joe, a passionate teacher and proud Native American. She reflected that:

> I learned about the Acoma People from the inside, not the stereotypes typically found in the Western culture. What I gleaned from those two weeks in New Mexico was more than learning how Acoma pottery was made but the closeness of a family and how they care for one another. I'm still marveling at how Daisy and Pearl have lived their lives with grace and respect. I'm grateful that there are individuals like Daisy and Pearl in this world to carry on and preserve the proud traditions of the Acoma people. (Rieser, personal notes, winter, 2003)

Cheryl Sloan wanted her students (grades 1-8) to make small, decorative bowls using the pinch pot method similar to how it is constructed by traditional Acoma potters, even while the students explored working with clay for the first time. She expected them to become familiar with the properties of clay as well as the sensuousness of how it feels, moves, and dries. From her experiences, she could share the "Historical hands-on exploration of pottery techniques used by the Acoma Pueblo" (Sloan, 2003, course work). Additionally, she valued the history that contextualized student production and expected her students to learn the part the Acoma People played in the history of the Southwest. She examined the influence of the Spanish on the Acoma People, analyzed information and understood the differences and similarities of the Native Americans of the Southwest.

Conclusion

Learning is not selective and is limited only by the individual. From my perspective, it was interesting that as these veteran teachers became students they exhibited the characteristics of any student in a foreign learning environment. It is insightful to understand how people are more similar than dissimilar, and regardless of maturity and experience, we all share similar reactions to environmental changes and differences in traditional classrooms. Hopefully, these teachers will understand their students better because of their own experiences of learning in a foreign environment. I believe that when teachers are students they become better teachers. The closer we all are to the center of learning, the more learning is facilitated. Sometimes a change of environment facilitates a radical learning curve.

In the learning environment, mutual respect must be present. As I talked with these teachers, they shared many insights, from the frustration of not being able to make a (good) seed pot to discovering that Grandma Daisy's (traditional) Chili was too hot to eat. Consistent with other trips was the uniform respect they all felt for Grandma Daisy and Aunt Pearl.

Through the gentle guidance of Grandma Daisy and Aunt Pearl, I watched the teachers' uncertainty be replaced with good-natured humor, gentle conversation, and authentic learning. It continues to impress me, as I reflect back on the journey, that they learned much more than the construction of Acoma pottery. They had learned to appreciate from a different perspective. The five full days of making traditional pottery was amazing. But, the saturation of the culture through learning about and preparing Acoma food, sharing humor and conversation, and listening to Grandma Daisy's and Aunt Pearl's stories had transformed anxiousness and doubt into calm reflection. When they were in doubt, they were assured. When they rushed, they were asked to relax and reflect. When they were proud, it was celebrated. Ram Dass (1985) wrote that the only thing a teacher can do is create an environment that is conducive to learning. Czyzewski's reflection echoes Dass:

> Daisy is simply amazing, as is her counterpart Pearl. These women never seemed annoyed with us, tired of our questions, irritated at our invasion of their home and lives, or bothered by our cultural ignorance. Perhaps this is the real reason I was supposed to come on this trip. I was supposed to witness and experience this patience and support firsthand, know how good

it feels to be treated as a person, and take that back to my students. When we didn't understand something, they didn't shriek "pay attention" or "next time don't talk while I give instructions." They simply repeated themselves time and time again all day long for five days. Neither one of them appeared irritated with our behavior although I am sure we broke more cultural rules than one could count. They were truly inspiring to me. (Czyzewski, personal notes, Summer 2003)

What is so invigorating to me is watching the dynamics of the group change as each person grew into a new perspective. The long 14-hour drive from Spring-field, the busy schedule of the home-life and the hectic pace of their Western world had been replaced by a subtle newness. On the Acoma Reservation, the Internet connection, the insistent telephone, and the barrage of television programs were replaced by hours of listening to traditional stories and learning about a culture while constructing just one more pot.

These teachers were freed from the moment to moment responsibilities that dominate most days. They made pots, talked, cooked, ate, listened, and most importantly, slowed down enough to appreciate. The journaling that was required for the course revealed not only the specific teaching of Grandma Daisy and Aunt Pearl, but the ability to reflect in a continuous and timely manner. These teachers slowed down enough to contemplate. They had the time.

Dewey (1934) reminds us that deep and durable learning comes from the ability to act, reflect, and react. These teachers had that time, time that many K-12 American students are not typically afforded. In the 21st century American schools, teachers and students are held to rigorous and rushed schedules to meet local, state, and national demands. While these teachers were at Acoma they relaxed into learning in contradiction to most of their students back in their home schools being rushed into learning as they move from class to class passing through crowded hallways. Lately, it seems that the paradigm for teaching is to do more, to be more accountable, and to give each student a broad, but general education. Frequently, I hear teachers comment that they do not have enough time to teach, much less, take the entire work home for grading. Per-haps, an alternative approach might be to do more in class and hold the indi-vidual student accountable by a focus approach to the subject and not allowing them to skim lightly over the content as they move quickly to a different task. Cultures define education differently, and in some, experience is more valuable than facts.

Perhaps it was the slower lifestyle of the reservation or perhaps it was the Acoma culture, but suddenly, time was available. I have often wondered if we would have a comprehensively better educational experience if we, as teachers, created an environment conducive to learning, provided for an authentic and creative moment, and expected our students to have the quality time to reflect on the holism of the interaction? I would like to think so. I would like to think that all people can link personal moments together to construct a string of cultural pearls to be appreciated and celebrated. I am convinced that this type of experience can be found in the inner city or rural school as well as on the reservation. It is our learning culture that should be shared with other people.

Author's Note

The research for this article originated with a Southwest Missouri State University *Funding For Results* grant written in collaboration with Dr. Billie Follensbee in 2001 that led to a trip in 2002 for undergraduate Art Historians (Art of the Native American Southwest, Art 496: Special Topics in Art History) directed by Dr. Billie Follensbee and for graduate Art Educators (Art of the Native American Southwest, ART 598: Special Topics in Art Education) directed by myself. Without this beginning collaboration and financial support, this research would have not been possible.

References

Barlett, D., & Steele, J. (2002). Wheel of misfortune. *Time Magazine, 160*(25), 44-58.

Dass, R. (1985). *Journey of awakening: A mediator's guidebook.* New York: Bantam Publishing.

Delacruz, E. M. (2003). Racism American style and resistance to change: Art education's role in the Indian mascot issue. *Art Education, 55*(3), 13-20.

Deloria, V. (1992). *God is red.* Golden, CO: Fulcrum Publishing.

Dewey, J. (1934). *Art as experience.* New York: Pedigree Publishing.

Hucko, B. (1999). *Art on the rocks: Rock art of the southwest.* Mariposa: Sierra Press.

Willis, S. (2003). Acoma pottery: First-hand experiences for art educators. *Teaching Artists Journal, 1*(4), 228-233.

Part II

Part II describes a number of intergenerational art programs across the United States in a variety of school and community settings. This section begins with a chapter by Gilden and Perlstein, coordinators of one of the leading intergenerational organizations in the country, Elders Share the Arts. They organize a variety of arts related programs throughout New York City involving professional artists, older adults, and elementary through high school students, integrating oral history with theatre, dance, music, writing and the visual arts. Next, Congdon, Underberg, and Van Wagenen link generations from a University of Central Florida film class, Jones High School, and Orange Center Elementary School to people in their community in order to collect stories and make documentary films and sculptures based on foods and other topics found to be interesting for students. Costanza follows by introducing a program at the Rogers School for Creative and Performing Arts, a magnet school in the Pittsburgh Public School District, serving grades six, seven, and eight, and their work with senior citizens from the community to produce intergenerational performances, narratives, and artwork. Alexenberg and Benjamin follow with a description of their Legacy Thrones program involving Hispanic, African American, and Jewish elders, work with high schools from the community and college art students from Jerusalem to create public art sculptures reflecting the cultural traditions and history of a community in Miami, Florida. Then, Barret identifies three intergenerational art programs in Northeast Georgia involving middle school students and older adults from local senior centers. The visual art forms introduced are: a history quilt, book arts, and photography based on themes of important places in the community, memories, and stories. The final chapter of the book identifies a museum-based art education program involving university students with children from the community in promoting intergenerational and interdisciplinary learning at the Tweed Museum of Art at the University of Minnesota in Duluth. All contributors to this section share a variety of possibilities that hope to inspire others to implement quality intergenerational partnerships with the many hidden educational resources in our communities.

7

*Marsha Gildin
and Susan Perlstein*

Community Connections:
Living History Arts

Elders Share the Arts (ESTA), founded in 1979, is dedicated to giving voice to
and advocating for the fullest possible involvement of elders in their central role
as conveyors of cultural heritage. In our community-based living history arts and
theatre programs, elders tell their culturally rich stories and share their life-
giving wisdom. Linking old and young, past informs future, the meaning and
purpose of life is reassessed and partnerships are forged as youth and elders
create living history artworks and performances. As participants plan, take part
and present together, they learn from each other's values, cultures, and histories.
ESTA helps to create a shared sense of history from which people can begin to
address their real needs and strengthen their communities.

ESTA uses arts, culture, and remembered history for youth and elders to
consider their individual and shared worlds and find common ground. The

democratic, artist-and-peer-led process creates safe spaces for honest discussion and exploration that nurtures open-ended fact finding, heart voicing, and synthesis. It builds trust between generations and cultures and links community organizations in partnership. And, truly, it highlights the remarkable talents, creativity, resilience, and strengths that reside within even the most unsung among us. This process is embodied in our core intergenerational programs.

In group art activities, participants learn to observe, share, explore, and create together. They learn *from and with* one another. ESTA's programs emphasize exploring commonalities and differences from a baseline of respect and appreciation. The journey through the art forms becomes an expression of what has been learned and shared. Through the artistic process, both young and old celebrate diversity through cultural expression and the animating of history *illuminated* through personal experience. Arts bring people together on common, opened, fertile ground.

Our living history arts programs partner children and youth with seniors to create collaborations based on their life stories learned through oral history interviews, reminiscence, and story swapping. Participants share experiences and stories about their heritages, life changes, and community issues that affect them. These stories serve as cornerstones to community building as people recognize their similarities and appreciate their differences. The relationships forged through this creative exchange extend dynamically into community life.

Based on their stories, people create an original art or theatre work for the entire community. The specific methods of program design and oral history interviewing techniques as well as the challenges of working with cross cultural issues is discussed in *Generating Community: Intergenerational Partnerships Through the Arts*, a book describing a successful community building model. *Legacy Works* addresses the transforming of life stories into visual arts projects. Both approaches will be discussed in this chapter.

Legacy Works and *Generating Community* start from the basis of valuing people's life experiences and knowing that there are stories waiting to be told, connected to, and shared. Although highlighting different art forms, visual and performance, the set-up, training, and intention of these programs reflect similar structural needs. Setting up partnerships, recruitment, and ongoing monitoring with clear communication help ensure program quality. We aim to create a safe space where story exchange on a personal and meaningful level can take place. Skills learning in the art forms, leading to artistic interpretations of shared stories culminate in a presentation or exhibit brought back to the community. A public presentation is crucial to the community building element of the projects. The presentations may be staged and/or exhibited at a school, senior center, community center, or at a central place such as a museum, library, theatre, or park. An evaluative process to help ensure program sustainability follows the culmination of the program.

Legacy Works

Legacy Works, a simple, flexible, yet powerful and profound program, transforms an elder person's life experiences into visual art: collage, photo-essay, memory box, or a variety of other types of artwork. The elder and youth who are trained in oral history interviewing and in visual art skills work together to create a vibrant, moving artwork that transmits the elder's personal and cultural history to the next generation. The finished artwork can be passed on to family, friends, or where the elder resides.

The basic model is exemplified by a program conducted at Union Settlement in East Harlem, Manhattan, with homebound elders and local teenagers recruited from Union's after-school youth services program. Thirty weeks long, the program was divided into six-month-long "modules." During the first week there were four training sessions (this was possible because the teens came every day to the after-school program for which they received community service learning credit). An artist trained by ESTA in oral history interviewing and group facilitation taught the teens oral history skills and gave them a general arts orientation. The subsequent four-week modules were each devoted to a different narrative theme and a different visual art form.

When the teens receive school credit, accountability is built in. Having a grade or community service learning credit based on their performance is an excellent mechanism for this. Schools require a portfolio of each student's work, including both art projects and their journals. The teacher uses the portfolio to assess the student's learning in the program. Senior and community centers may only want a report based on the survey information, or they may request a record of attendance, skills learned, and works produced. Essential to the success of the program is having a central site where the teens can check in before and after each session.

At Union Settlement, in the first module, the theme was family history and the form was collage. In week one, during a three-hour training session, the teenagers learned to make a family tree (by making one of their own) and developed the family history theme. Once a week for the next three weeks, the teens met at Union Settlement for a brush-up session on the skills they had learned, and then went in pairs to visit neighborhood elders, bringing their trees as samples. (Since many of the elders were initially fearful of being alone with the teens, we made sure that a home health aide was present in each elder's home during these visits, which lasted an hour and a half.)

85

Elders who live alone are often mistrustful of people ringing their doorbell. They also may forget about their appointment. They need to be reminded that the students are coming. Once there, sometimes the elders are reluctant to let the teenagers *leave* and try to get them to stay longer. Students need to know they have a place to call if any problem arises. It is important for the senior administrator to maintain a relationship with the seniors as a way to check up.

On the first visit, the teens conducted the oral-history interview. On the second, they helped the elder collect memorabilia—personal photographs or other items reflecting the elder's family history—or evocative images from magazines or other sources. On the third visit, teens and elders together used these items to create the elder's own family tree. Since many of the seniors were Latino immigrants and the youth were children of immigrants, you can imagine what a fruitful interchange about life experiences resulted. After each visit, the youth returned to Union Settlement for a group evaluation and discussion of their

Figure: 7.1

experiences with the elders.

The next month, we repeated this process with another visual art form. In addition to collage, the projects included block prints, memory boxes, and relief sculpture. Themes included immigrating to America, childhood memories, and neighborhood reminiscences. Finally, the elders and teens selected the finished works they wanted hung in a month-long exhibition at Union Settlement's

Community Gallery. The youth learned how to mount and hang the art, as well as create and distribute flyers. Union Settlement ambulated the elders to the gala opening celebration, where elders and youth spoke publicly about their experience together.

One teenager, Rosa, visited Marie, who at 87 was frail and had severe arthritis. On her first visit, Rosa discovered that like herself, Marie was part Puerto Rican and part African American. Since Marie had difficulty drawing the details in her family tree, she asked Rosa for help. They drew thick roots in deep umber, branches covered with forest-green leaves, and scarlet birds flying away in a blue sky. In the process, Rosa learned that they shared a common desire to move to a warmer, more welcoming place. As the program continued, Rosa began to confide in Marie, who looked forward to her coming. Gradually, over time, Marie became Rosa's surrogate grandmother. They began busily collecting stories, photos, and sayings for a collage. Marie, who said she had learned to trust herself from her grandmother in Puerto Rico, passed on this counsel to Rosa. After the program ended Rosa remained close to Marie and continued to visit her. Before she went away to college, she brought her younger sister, who carried on the visits with Marie.

The youth services coordinator reported that the kids developed not only friendships among themselves, but a wonderful relationship with the seniors and learned about artmaking. She said:

> The seniors loved the program. They said it gave them something to look forward to each week. They felt less isolated, and had more community support—for them it was like getting fresh air. And I saw the kids change and grow. Sometimes, their school grades improved. Now, when they walk down the street, they're a lot more considerate and compassionate to seniors they pass by than before. They feel important, that they're doing something that is good for their lives and for the seniors' lives. The seniors give them a lot of friendship. The kids feel needed and appreciated, and they feel they have a niche here, and community support. This was a real change from the beginning of the program, when there was a lot of mistrust and misconceptions between the teens and seniors.

The culmination of *Legacy Works*, the event that confirms and reinforces the community created through art, is the public exhibition and celebration of the participants' achievements. Curating means selecting the works to be exhibited, giving them titles, creating wall placards, and deciding how the works will be arranged. In most cases this is the arts coordinator's job. The opening of the exhibition should be a reception with a ceremony whose centerpiece is the elders and helpers standing up together to tell about their experience of the artmaking. Generally, the project director is in charge of all aspects of this event, except for the curating. Another important job is drawing up a list of community newspapers and writing a press release to send to the editors. When *Legacy Works* includes students who are receiving community-service learning credit, certificates of credit or completion are given out at this ceremony.

Evaluation is conducted after the exhibition and summarizes the total program, bringing together all of the documentation. The main component of the evaluation is a survey of all the program participants. We interview staff, youth, and elders in person, by phone, or in a group setting. In general, a *Legacy Works* program can go wrong in two ways: interpersonally and logistically. Breakdowns occur when, for example, the pairings between youth and elders aren't working, or an administrator is not available when needed.

It's important to keep in mind the overall purpose of *Legacy Works*—to build community by developing partnerships across institutions and age groups. It works because creative expression is at the heart of successful community building.

Generating Community

Generating Community is a program consisting of weekly workshop sessions which bring seniors in senior center, community centers, and/or geriatric centers together with children and youth ranging in age from elementary to high school, in order to build community through living history theatre. Each program lasts about 26 sessions. ESTA artists train the group in interviewing skills and sensory associations in order to gather life experiences from *both* the elders and the youth. Separate orientation sessions are held with elders and youth to explore ideas or stereotypes one group may have about the other. What do you think of when you hear the word *old* or *elder*? How about *youth, kid,* or *teenagers*? It is important to air, acknowledge, and discuss these associations before the groups meet.

When the two groups come together, it is a period of *getting to know you*, facilitated through activities that gently open people up to one another: share the story of your name, bring in a family photograph, explore one another's hands and tell a story of something your hands have done—gather the responses into a group poem, get into small groups, and talk about your favorite foods or about family holidays! Warming a group up to itself is the preamble for interviewing and story swapping. If safety, friendliness, and respect are felt within the group, stories of personal meaning will come forward—everything from humorous to poignant to instructive. The ESTA artist is trained to listen for themes that emerge. These themes, unique to each group, become the shaping threads for living history arts such as stories from the neighborhood, stories of courage, immigration, work, family, traditions, and values.

Flushing, Queens, is one of the fastest changing immigrant communities in all of New York City, home to immigrants from over 80 countries. For 15 years ESTA has been conducting intergenerational programs at the Selfhelp Benjamin

Rosenthal Senior Center, a center founded with reparations monies to serve immigrant Holocaust survivors. In the last decade, the neighborhood has changed tremendously, expanding to include many newcomers from all parts of Asia, Africa, Eastern Europe, and Central and South America. The elders who volunteer in the program are lively and committed. They range in age from 65-92 and are predominantly Jewish.

Public School 24, an elementary school around the corner, has partnered with ESTA and the senior center for ten years. P.S. 24, once an Arts Magnet School for Authors and Illustrators, specializes in literacy and literature. The oral history and storytelling approach used by ESTA fits well with the school's curriculum goals. Program planning between the ESTA artist and the classroom teacher ensures this alignment. In addition, the participating 5th grade music class compliments the exuberant song and performance enthusiasts at the senior center volunteering for the intergenerational program. Funding to support the intergenerational program comes from the school's Project Arts budget, the senior center and the local Flushing councilman's office. Buy-in from all partners and the community was agreed upon and is essential for a successful program.

A narrative followed the development of the Flushing intergenerational living history theatre program. It was Tuesday morning, October 2, 2001, at 9:45 and class 5-328 was walking from their school around the corner to the senior center. They were looking forward to their first meeting with the elders. The students brought with them their newly constructed ESTA journals in which they kept weekly entries of reactions, reflections, assignments, and stories all related to their time together with the seniors. More than half the students were immigrants, some as recently as last month, and others from years before.

Exactly three weeks earlier, two planes crashed into the World Trade Towers and everyone's lives changed. In the ESTA planning meeting, the seniors voiced great concern. They wanted the children to know that they were safe, respected, and cared for in their community. The seniors did not want to avoid speaking about 9-11. They felt the children needed to speak about it as well, but they did not want to frighten them. What theme could emerge out of such a time together?

The "getting to know you" period evolved with gentle enthusiasm. Introductions, playful name games, family photographs, and group poems were shared as well as questions and experiences around 9-11. The question arose, "Who or what helps you in scary times?" The children and elders interviewed one another on someone who inspired them in their lives. From the interviews the children made a class newspaper in cartoon form and distributed copies throughout the senior center. Further exploration of this question evoked in the elders remembrances and stories of World War II where qualities of camaraderie and gestures of friendship were life altering.

HEADLINE: GRANDPA SAYS, BALANCE YOUR PRIORITIES!
HEADLINE: YOU CAN LEARN A LOT FROM A FRIEND
HEADLINE: GOBBLE! GOBBLE! TURKEYS ON THE MOVE
SERVE THEIR COUNTRY WELL.

Figure: 7.2

The elders interviewed the children on their experiences of 9-11. The children gave headlines to the day:

HEADLINE: ATTACK SHOCKS THE WORLD
HEADLINE: THE TWINS ARE GONE
HEADLINE: STRANGERS BECOME HEROES
HEADLINE: WE ARE ONE

With stories from World War II and a tribute to 9-11, a performance piece took shape. Scenes were built through improvisation, songs were chosen, and voice was given to what holds people and communities together in difficult times.
The living history theatre presentation was called: "Light the Fire Within: Stories of Inspiration," and was based on a story of the United States Olympic Committee's search for torch bearers—an event that actually took place and passed through Flushing that year. For the performance piece, the Committee encouraged the general public to submit stories of inspiration. Stories poured in. Certain stories, once announced in headline form, came alive and were enacted. Scene One was

Figure: 7.3

called "The Inspiration of Camaraderie." Al told the story of camaraderie with his fellow soldiers during World War II. A Thanksgiving Day meal was interrupted because the troops needed to march to the waiting war ships. They decided to march while passing the food over their heads to one another while chanting, "Turkey here! Gravy, please! Pumpkin pie, and I don't lie!" As Al added poignantly, some buddies made it home from the war while others did not. In Scene Two, "The Inspiration Of Friendship," Kay, as a young new wife, left New York and all she knew to follow her husband down to boot camp during the war. Their new landlady befriended Kay by letting a chick hatch in the warmth of her hand. They all became her best daily companions during her time down South. In Scene Three, "Tribute to 9/11: Strangers Become Heroes," The Olympic committee recognized the inspiration and sacrifice of everyday people. The students and seniors formed a tableau to honor and thank all the people who helped out on that day. Actors stepped out and announced a series of headlines that described heroic acts and enormous losses from September 11, 2001.

The performance piece held heart and humor. Performances at the school and senior center were announced in the local papers and opened to the entire community. Family, friends, politicians, and funders were invited. A collective effort became a collective retelling and honoring. People felt safety, respect, and caring in their community.

Evaluation of such programs comes from final reports and interviews conducted by each partner, survey/evaluations filled out by participants, from writings and thank you cards, and from the testimony of a final wrap-up session with all participants documented by the ESTA artist. Some comments were:

> My experience with the seniors was great. I felt happy with them working on the show. Some of them even said we were like their children. That was true. They were like grandparents. They told us their past and how their life was. We told them about our life. (Bhavesh, student)

> Everyone says what we do for them, but what I feel is what they do for us. I know I have grown from this experience. I always stayed within my own culture, but things are changing now. I've learned from the children about their cultures. I've learned to understand them. I don't think I would have without this group. (Estelle, senior)

> As a parent, it is so moving to me to see how far we have all come. I know this has meant so much to my daughter. When we go shopping at Bravo Foods, she goes running to look down every aisle in hopes of seeing the seniors she knows. I can't thank you all enough. (Denise, parent)

As illustrated by these two programs, *Legacy Works* and *Generating Community*, intergenerational arts that stem from life story and the transformation of those stories into visual and performance art forms are excellent ways to build community. The creative process of living history presentations lead people to understand and empathize with each other, have fun learning new skills together and discover new ways of communicating. Living history arts programs are cost-effective, efficient, and afford a natural way to reconnect youth and elders, family and community—the basic building blocks of every society.

References

Brown, C. S. (1988). *Like it was: A complete guide for writing oral history*. New York: Teachers and Writers Collaborative.

Davis, S., & Ferdman, B. (1993). *Nourishing the heart: A guide to intergenerational arts projects in the schools*. New York: City Lore, Incorporated, and Creative Ways.

Golden, S., & Perlstein, S. (2002). *Legacy works: Transforming memory into visual arts*. New York: National Center for Creative Aging/ESTA.

Larson, R. (2004). *A stage for memory: A guide to the living history theater program of Elders Share the Arts*. New York: National Center for Creative Aging/ESTA.

Perlstein, S., & Bliss, J. (1994). *Generating community: Intergenerational partnerships through the expressive arts*. New York: Elders Share the Arts.

8

Kristin G. Congdon,
Natalie Underberg,
and Sterling Van Wagenen

Linking Generations Through Film And Foodways

Project Overview

In Fall 2002, the Heritage Alliance in the University of Central Florida's (UCF) School of Film and Digital Media began an intergenerational project that linked numerous African American and Haitian youth with their ancestors. Filmmaker Sterling Van Wagenen and art educator/folklorist Kristin Congdon coordinated the project. Folklorist Natalie Underberg was responsible for many of the day-to-day administrative and programmatic aspects of the project. Funded by a Community Higher Education School Partnership grant (CHESP) from Florida's Department of Education, this service-learning project used the arts to explore information about traditional foodways[1] experienced in Orlando's downtown Parramore area. Besides UCF students, this project involved youth from Jones High School, children from Orange Center Elementary School, the Black

Veterans Association[2], the Soldiers to Scholars Program[3], Queen Bee's Soul Food Restaurant in Parramore, and the UCF Office of Diversity Initiatives. Early work included the planning and implementation of a series of artists' workshops aimed at motivating students to begin thinking about favorite foods and the ways in which they are presented and served. In the Spring of 2003 UCF students enrolled in an advanced documentary course team taught by Van Wagenen and Underberg. The course textbook was *Food in the USA* (2002).

Documenting foodways was selected as a topic for the class because everyone can easily tell stories about food. These stories are often powerful in that they reveal aspects of tradition and community identity. Giving this topic to the filmmakers relieved the university students of one major part of the filmmaking process that can delay completion of a film, or worse, cause a student to give up all together. This topic also supports the cries of numerous art educators that artmaking be relevant to its context. While food may or may not be considered an art form (it certainly has an aesthetic dimension and the presentation of it often deals with the visual), it succeeds as an artistic subject that easily explores community-based information. Decades ago, McFee (1966) and Chalmers (1978, 1981) asked that we ground our art studies in context, using anthropology and the ethnographic method as a way to approach it. Chalmers wrote that the study of art needs to examine "the values and beliefs of society and its changing institutions, communities, and group relationships" (p. 12). Building on the research of McFee and Chalmers, Congdon (1986, 1987) identifies varying ways to explore tradition in folk art as well as approaches to incorporate folk speech in art dialogue. Our foodways project was built on this research, demonstrating how theory works in practice.

Intergenerational folklife educational projects have a number of benefits. Hamer (2000) identifies five outcomes. From her list, all five apply to our foodways project. They are: (a) valuing everyday artistic expressions, (b) instilling pride in the family and local community, (c) challenging the dualistic authority of elite and popular culture, (d) recognizing and celebrating the everyday person as a teacher, and (e) promoting collaborative action. Increasingly folklorists are successfully working in educational settings. Grider (1995) recognizes that there is a vast audience interested in learning about folklore and calls for more interdisciplinary work with those in other disciplines. Our foodways project incorporated skills from various disciplines including folklore, creative and ethnographic writing, social studies, performance, and art forms such as drawing, painting, sculpture, and filmmaking. In many respects the well known Foxfire Project served as a model (Wiggington, 1972).

This project was based on a cascading model of service learning, a particularly powerful paradigm for engaging youth as well as linking generations (see

Justinianno & Scherer 2001; Devitas, et al., 1998). Underberg began by teaching UCF students the basics of ethnographic fieldwork. These students, in turn, taught ethnographic skills to K-12 students. The training included a basic introduction to foodways, focusing on the traditionality of foodways as a component of folklore. This information was followed by an introduction to interviewing techniques, working with a "script" that breaks the process into before, during, and after the interview, and engaging in role-playing an interview. Effective training in ethnographic and folkloristic interviewing includes Ives' (1980) and Spradley's (1997) guidelines for establishing rapport, showing genuine interest, and "thickening" the information received by, for example, asking follow-up questions. In addition, particular insights from recent scholarship on sociolinguistic and feminist approaches to ethnographic interviewing were introduced. These included learning to frame interviews by using the informants' own communication style and utilizing a more discussion-oriented style in place of demanding that the informant "take the floor" (see Briggs, 1986; Gluck & Patai, 1991). (This approach is in keeping with Congdon's 1986 suggestion that folk speech be used when studying artwork.) Then, film students led folklore fieldwork workshops. Students from Jones High School and Orange Center then interviewed community members, often parents, as well as each other, to elicit recipes and stories about foodways. Follow-up workshops were also held which allowed K-12 students to practice their newly acquired skills. During these workshops students interviewed members of the Black Veterans Association. K-12 students practiced interviewing techniques with members of the Association, learning about, for example, veterans' nostalgic longing for mom's special baked chicken.

The folklore fieldwork workshops were modeled on Folklife Institutes offered by the Department of State, Florida Folklife Program. They offer a layperson's introduction to identifying and documenting folklife traditions. They enable everyone to become folklorists/ethnographers, thus empowering people to appreciate and understand their own traditions as well as those of others. For university students, first learning and then having to teach basic ethnographic methods both reinforces the lessons learned in the classroom and prepares them to successfully conduct documentary research work. In addition, the folklore fieldwork model, focusing on ethnographic interviewing, offers K-12 students and community members an ideal way to bridge the generations. Young and old can interact by focusing on discussions about traditions—both current and from the past.

Foodways

Foodways was selected as a topic for our project, in part, because it is relevant to all age groups. Additionally, it is something about which we all have experience and knowledge. Information about it can be collected relatively easily in both formal and informal settings, and it is a seemingly "trivial" topic that addresses profound themes. Foodways practices and stories share certain common themes across generations and ethnicities that serve to show participants that people are the same, yet different—for example, the idea that certain family members know how to add "that special touch." A focus on foodways, with its dual everyday and yet culturally meaningful nature, offers an ideal way to engage students and their families in school projects. In addition, foodways represents a generally nonthreatening topic through which to establish trust and rapport, thus offering university and K-12 students and African-American and Afro-Caribbean groups a venue for relating to one another.

Perhaps most significantly, foodways offers a concrete, easy-to-grasp way for students and others to understand key issues of cultural heritage and tradition. As the project revealed, traditional foodways plays a number of roles in community life; food symbolizes emotion, marks social roles in a family, evokes nostalgia, demonstrates challenges to successful food preparation, and transmits knowledge from person to person. For instance, one Parramore story illustrates how a traditional Haitian dish called *griot* was traditional in one girl's family in two ways. When her mother made it she both passed on a Haitian foodways tradition and at the same time created a family tradition by cooking it to mark special occasions.

Filmmaking

As the K-12 students were creating artwork based on the stories they found, the film students were asked to make 10-minute films based on what they discovered working with the youth. The 10-minute limit was intended to discourage excessive ambition in attempting too much and to pressure the student to focus on the quality of the storytelling, rather than the amount of footage photographed.

This folklore/filmmaking partnership was particularly timely and appropriate because storytelling is a foundational element in the education of UCF film students. With recent revisions in the department's curriculum, the faculty wisely understood that good filmmakers are, first and foremost, good storytellers, and that the discipline of recognizing and structuring stories is one which must be made explicit in the students' academic experience. With that emphasis already present in the curriculum, the additional ethnographic training techniques used by folklorists, and often by art educators, was seen as a natural extension (really a deepening) of the film student's experience. Certainly, we had in mind words from historian Joy Hakim's 1997 speech as she accepted the Michener Prize in Writing: "It is the storyteller's job to make the world around us understandable. . . . Finding the story in a subject is to discover its essence. If we can train our students to pattern the world into stories we can turn them into powerful, analytical learners" (Hakim, 2003).

The fifteen students were in their second or third year in the film program, with experience using digital camera and non-linear (computer) editing systems. Their familiarity with the technology made it possible to focus completely on story training and the documentary process. Given the obstacle of not completing the films, all common to student films, the decision to use more experienced students was vindicated many times.

We recognized that gaining access to the often-closed circles of individual families and émigré cultures is a challenge, even for an experienced, professional filmmaker. Documentary filmmakers are viewed as both a source of fascination in our media-saturated culture and also a threat to privacy and the closely guarded comfort of our modes of self-presentation. This obstacle is especially difficult to surmount for the student filmmaker who is often uncertain about his or her technical skills and the challenges of making coherent stories out of unpredictable, immediate circumstances. An intended consequence of using foodways was to provide the students with a topic that was easy to talk about and certain to generate many stories. It functioned to create a relatively safe and immediate bond of trust between the *insiders* and the *outsiders* that would give the filmmakers an entry point into the younger student's lives and families. Many of the university students, in fact, developed significant bonds of trust with their elementary or high school counterparts. It was interesting to note that this bond was so strong for many of the filmmakers that they were unable to see possible negative aspects of their subject's stories as they began shooting. There was a significant degree of self-censorship in exploring all aspects of the specific stories they chose. This problem led us to substantial discussions about the ethics of documentary filmmaking and the responsibility filmmakers have to their subjects and their "objectivity."

Student films were to be shown in a public community presentation at the end of the semester. Beyond this culminating event, we also expected that the films would be an on going catalyst for discussions both within the families involved and the schools.

Within our two public schools, elementary students were selected from the fourth and fifth grades, and high school students from the eleventh and twelfth. Because of scheduling problems at the high school, the most consistent ethnographic work took place in the elementary school. The students met after school in their media center with the film students for the workshops. As this process progressed, the film students began to find aspects of the children's lives that

97

were instinctively attractive to them. Some filmmakers were taken home to meet the children's parents; others were introduced to trusted playmates; and others, always in teams, continued to work with individual children.[4]

One UCF student became interested in what it means to be a foster child. Another recognized the preoccupation of elementary teachers and students with an imminent (and controversial) state test, the Florida Comprehensive Assessment Test (FCAT). Still another student was attracted, initially, to the food traditions of a Nigerian émigré family and this interest in food grew into a precise little vignette on the meaning of hope and determination. One filmmaker grew worried about the daily safety of her mentoree, and explored the children's attitudes about physical and metaphysical safety. Yet another student discovered a grandmother who had refined the art of living joyfully from finding and reusing the detritus of our consumer culture. Two film students teamed together to explore a family gospel church, and two others the hopes and dreams of a single mother sacrificing a singing career for the sake of her three children.

Because of scheduling difficulties at the high school level, only one project emerged from this context. After an initial story training meeting with a group of students, one UCF filmmaker became intrigued with the girl's basketball team (hardly a foodways subject), and began to attend practices. The resulting film was a rough, but heartbreaking account of her team's drive for a state championship; the final version was twenty minutes long, and only roughly edited, but so accurately envisioned that content triumphed over form. This project taught us that, though we had intended all the films to be focused on foodways, once the process of inter-personal connections began between the university students and their subjects, the water, so-to-speak, found its own channel. We judged that it would be counterproductive to redirect a filmmaker's passionate interest in an aspect of their subjects' lives in favor of a rigidly enforced topic. All the UCF students, working either individually or in teams, completed films.

Each student completed a final evaluation of the experience. The majority remarked, in various ways, on their discovery of the common struggle all human beings have, regardless of background. One clear outcome for the fledgling documentarians was an increase in self-confidence as filmmakers and as individuals. At the beginning of this project, all but three of the students were extremely nervous about entering into the private lives of others, and certainly wary of how they would be accepted in cultures very different from their own. (One student, in fact, was so anxious about the prospect of culturally working outside his comfort zone that he dropped the class after the initial meeting with the elementary students.) In recognizing the common bonds between human beings that makes this kind of work possible, they discovered, more specifically, how crucial two qualities were in the making of their films: trustworthiness and a clear point-of-view.

A second outcome was an appreciation for the amount of work that it takes to "find the story." Many of the students assumed that merely by going to a location and shooting footage of external events, they would be able to edit together a coherent and interesting film. They soon discovered that good filmmaking, like good storytelling, involves a discipline of *seeing*, i.e., an explicit and intuitive method of gathering together the research, the technology, the unpredictability of behavior, and the filmmaker's own personality into a process that, though dependent on external events, reveals the hidden life of the subject with compassion and fairness.

From the community perspective, the elementary students, their families, and teachers had an opportunity to get a fresh sense of important, but often unappreciated aspects of their lives. For example, one teacher was surprised at how much her students worried about the future of the school if they failed the FCAT exam. One 4th grader, for instance, was convinced that if she and her peers failed to pass the test, the school would be torn down. A parent was surprised at how open and conversational his son was on camera in light of his sullen behavior at home. For others, like the self-sacrificing mother, the film was a way of acknowledging her value in the community, of publicly recognizing that she was, indeed a good mother. And a city councilwoman who attended the final community presentation was impressed by the commitment and sensitivity of these "outsiders" in understanding the people in her district.

In addition to the public presentation at a community center in the Parramore district, which concluded the formal part of the project, the films were or will be shown at the annual UCF Film School Industry Screening, the WellsBuilt Museum of African American History in Orlando, and on the local PBS affiliate station.

Other Artwork and Outcomes

Zines, which are mini-magazines, were also highlighted as a student activity. The form of a zine was selected because it allows for multiple combinations of writing, drawing, and collaging. Students were encouraged to meld images and text in a free-form and intuitive manner. Images could be either original or appropriated from a variety of sources (Congdon & Blandy, 2003). This format was selected for our elementary and secondary students, because it was a less structured way of expressing themselves than they generally experience in school. Local artists visited the schools to lead workshops during which elementary and high school students created artwork about foodways. This artwork involved many kinds of media and writing. Several different approaches were used: making three-dimensional representations of favorite traditional meals, creating potato-stamp borders with food narratives in the middle, and constructing mosaics of favorite foods.

The artwork was combined with recipes and contextual storytelling information to create a collaborative desktop publication that was distributed to project participants and local archives. The publication was divided into several sections reflecting the project results: African American "Soul Food," Caribbean Cooking, Staple Foods, Everyday and Fantasy Dishes, and That "Special" Touch. Students wrote about the food they loved, foods they hated, and foods they enjoy eating with family and friends.

The cascading service-learning model that was used benefited each group of participants in different ways. For UCF students, the project offered an opportunity to apply theories and concepts learned in class in a real-world setting. It reinforced their learning of ethnographic skills by teaching them to younger students, and by facilitating workshops they enacted the critical step in ethnographic research of establishing rapport. For students at Orange Center Elementary and Jones High, the project provided a needed opportunity for positive mentoring by university students. Many of these students have had no previous contact with the university, and by being able to work together with college students on a service-learning project, they were better able to see themselves as future college students.

In addition to bringing university and K-12 schools together, this project built bridges between schools and the wider community. Students, school faculty, family, and other sectors of the community needed to work together to ensure the project's success. For example, having African-American veterans share their experiences with young students enriched the project. Hosting the public event at a nearby senior center would not have been possible without the support of the City of Orlando staff and board members who waived the fee to use the site. Making this request strengthened the partnership between the university and the city.

Besides viewing the films, the public event included a presentation of food stories and recipes collected by Orange Center Elementary and Jones High School students. University and K-12 students collaborated to select and prepare the public presentation of their collected recipes and stories, thus providing additional mentoring opportunities. Students performed stories about topics such as Haitian griot and memories of the Navy. UCF students also helped to market the event by distributing a full-color invitation to several hundred people.

The attendees, including K-12 students, their teachers and families, and members of the community, enjoyed foods prepared from collected recipes such as Peach Cobbler, Curry Chicken and Dumplings, and boiled plantains. During the second half of the program, UCF students introduced their films, and the whole community watched the compilation documentary. A special effort was made to ensure that students and their families involved in the making of these films were in attendance and seated with the student filmmakers. Finally, UCF students videotaped the event to create a lasting record of the project. The event was intentionally held at a nearby senior center to reinforce the community foundations of the project.

Besides benefiting UCF filmmaking students in ways that have already been noted, the project positively impacted other participants and the Orlando community in a number of ways. For the K-12 students the project increased self-confidence about their heritage and prospects for school success. Students who had been labeled "at-risk" committed to the project and owned it. The project also brought the community together around a celebration of local traditions. The foodways topic provided a positive way for African-American and Afro-Caribbean members of the community to interact.

Ethnographic-based service-learning projects provide an ideal way to engage students of all ages in topics of culture and community. Like other folklife-in-education programs such as Foxfire or *Louisiana Voices* (available online at: http://www.louisianavoices.org/edu_home.html), the CHESP Foodways project connects school and community through primary research and direct experience with living traditions rooted in local culture. Contextualized art experiences are used to help individuals across generations and cultures interact and celebrate differences and commonalties. Additionally, educational anthropologists assert that when students see their cultures reflected in the curriculum, the gap between school and home culture is diminished, thus increasing a student's engagement with school. The cascading service-learning model used in the CHESP Foodways project, moreover, establishes a concrete way for different generations and sectors of the community to work collaboratively and draw on the strengths of each group.

Finally, this project has been a major factor in helping us formulate the UCF Heritage Alliance, a research and project-based organization that works on heritage-based educational projects that utilize technology. It provided a specific project to help us begin building lasting partnerships with area organizations as it demonstrated, once again, the power of storytelling and the arts.

References

Briggs, C. (1986). *Learning how to ask: A sociolinguistic appraisal of the role of the interview in social science research.* New York: Cambridge University Press.

Chalmers, F. G. (1978). Teaching and studying art history: Some anthropological and sociological considerations. *Studies in Art Education, 20*(1), 18-25.

Chalmers, F. G. (1981). Art education as ethnology. *Studies in Art Education, 22*(3), 6-14.

Congdon, K. G. (1986). The meaning and use of folk speech in art criticism. *Studies in Art Education, 27*(3), 140-148.

Congdon, K. G. (1987). Toward a theoretical approach to the study of folk art: A definition. *Studies in Art Education, 28*(2), 93-106.

Congdon, K. G., & Blandy, D. (2003). Using zines to teach about postmodernism and the communication of ideas. *Art Education, 56*(3), 43-52.

Counihan, C. (2002). *Food in the USA.* New York: Routledge.

Devitas, J., Johns, R., Simpson, D., & Simon, D. (Eds.). (1998). *To serve and learn: The spirit of community in liberal education.* New York: Peter Lang.

Gluck, S., & Patai, D. (1991). *Women's words: The feminist practice of oral history.* New York: Routledge.

Grider, S. (1995). Passed down from generation to generation. *Journal of American Folklore, 108*(428), 178-185.

Hakim, J. (2003). *1997 Acceptance speech for the Michener Prize in Writing.* Retrieved from http://gos.sbc.edu/h/hakim.html

Hamer, L. (2000). Folklore in schools and multicultural education: Toward institutionalizing noninstitutional knowledge. *Journal of American Folklore, 113*(447), 44-69.

Ives, E. (1980). *The tape-recorded interview: A manual for field workers in folklore and oral history.* Knoxville: University of Tennessee Press.

Justinianno, J., & Scherer, C. (2001). *Youth voice: A guide for engaging youth in leadership and decision-making in service-learning programs.* Washington, D C: Points of Light Foundation.

Louisiana Division of the Arts. (2003). *Louisiana Voices Folklife in Education Project.* Retrieved from http://www.louisianavoices.org/edu_home.html

McFee, J. K. (1966). Society, art and education. In E. L. Mattill (Ed.), *A seminar for research in art education* (pp. 122-140). University Park, PA: The Pennsylvania State University.

Spradley, J. (1997). *The ethnographic interview.* Florence, KY: International Thomson Publishing.

Wiggington, E. (1972). *The Foxfire book.* New York: Anchor.

Endnotes

[1]*Foodways* is a term used by folklorists to designate the cultural context in which traditional food is prepared, shared, and appreciated. In some cases it can extend to the way in which the food is gathered.

[2]The Black Veterans Association, led by Orlando residents Troy Demps and Alzo Reddick, is an official partner of the American Folklife Center's Veterans History Project, mandated by Congress to record the experiences of those who served our country during wartime.

[3]The Soldiers to Scholars Program, directed by Alzo Reddick at UCF, helps former active military members to transition to the university environment through programs including mentoring opportunities.

[4]As part of the filmmakers' preparation in class, we introduced formal training in diversity and established "rules" for working with individual children, one of which was always to work in a team when with a single child. Also, each filmmaker had to submit a "volunteer application" to Orlando's Orange County School District, and was subject to background checks before working with the school.

9

Pamela Costanza

The Creative And Performing Arts As A Generational Bridge

Using the Visual and Performing Arts as a Generational Bridge

The Rogers Middle School for Creative and Performing Arts, a magnet school in Pittsburgh, Pennsylvania, coordinates an intergenerational, interdisciplinary arts exhibit and performance annually involving middle school faculty, students, and senior citizens from the community. The arts and academic teachers select a program theme each year inspired by local and national events. The visual art, media, and creative writing departments each organize opportunities for students to interview and discuss relevant topics with elders in the community. The experience is documented through photography, drawing, and writing by teams composed of both young and older adult participants. Meanwhile, the dance, vocal, and instrumental music departments work closely with students and elders in the community to create a performance related to the same theme. The intergenerational exchanges between middle school students and older adults become bridges for understanding the histories and cultures represented within the multiethnic diversity of the Pittsburgh community. The final art exhibit and performance bring parents, members of the community, the middle school faculty and students, and senior citizen participants together for an educational and uplifting experience, culminating with lasting bonds between generations.

Planning and Process

Planning for the intergenerational program begins with the selection of a theme by the middle school arts and academic teachers based on its educational value and its ability to encourage discussion and synergy between the generations. In early September, the arts and academic teachers that wish to take part in the intergenerational project meet to brainstorm for theme ideas. The theme changes each year, inspired by current events in the nation and the community. Once the theme is developed, a meeting is held with staff members from local community senior citizen centers willing to participate. Responsibilities are assigned for the following necessities: (a) finding a sponsor to donate the location for the performance and exhibit; (b) creating and printing the keepsake booklets and programs; (c) creating, printing, and mailing invitations; and (d) planning and setting up a reception to follow the performance and exhibit.

The teachers and senior center staff discuss possible sites and schedule dates for the performance and exhibit. To best share the educational experience with the public, we look for sites for the performance and exhibit in a variety of public venues, from museums, banks, auditoriums, office building foyers, to local colleges and universities. Once the location is determined, the request is made to provide the location to our project, free of charge. As of this date, our request has never been denied, once the project is explained to them.

Program dates and times are determined with the consideration of the site location and the participants. A calendar is agreed upon by all participants including: (a) when seniors will come to the school to meet with the various arts groups to plan and rehearse for the performance and exhibit; (b) a deadline for when the artwork, photographs, and writings should go to the printer for the keepsake booklet; (c) a time when the invitations need to be made, printed and mailed; and (d) the date, time and place for the art exhibit and performance.

Arts Creating & Rehearsals

Creating

The visual art, media, and creative writing departments begin to outline their strategy based on the theme of the year. In each area, students and senior citizens create an individual piece that will be included in the keepsake booklet as well as be matted and placed on display in the exhibit. Sometimes, slides of individual work are projected as a backdrop during parts of the performance. Based on the theme, students and seniors will be involved in research around different artists, styles, symbols, and community ethnic and cultural histories.

Pittsburgh Past & Present

Figure: 9.1. Pittsburgh Past & Present. (1998). Keepsake booklet, including photographs and artwork from students and senior citizens, Gary Dawson, Brianna Smith, Alecia Shipman, Michele McGraw, Christopher St. Pierre, Rachel Sam, Chase Campbell, Paul McRoberts, and Nathan Howard.

Within the visual art area, students and seniors created an *interpretive* piece of artwork that best represented the theme. Students and seniors were able to select from watercolors, acrylics, colored pencils, markers, and technical drawing pens to express their ideas. After meeting to discuss ideas, media students and senior citizens went on a photo outing in the community to capture images related to the theme. In recent years, with the onset of digital photography, students have been able to teach the senior citizens how to use the computer to enhance the digital images from the photo outing. Creative writing students interviewed seniors and discussed various points of view based on the theme. Students then created one-page narratives, stories, and poems based on their conversations with senior citizens.

PITTSBURGH NEIGHBORHOODS, PEOPLE AND CULTURES

Figure: 9.2. Pittsburgh Neighborhoods, People and Cultures. (1999).
Keepsake booklet, including artwork by Andrew Janicki, student.

Development of a Theme

The following illustrations are program covers from past performances. Each cover includes the titles of the various themes and reasons for their development. The program covers also include samples of the artwork and/or photographs from each exhibit.

Pittsburgh Past & Present (see Figure 9.1). After viewing archival photographs of Pittsburgh from the Carnegie Museum of Art, students and senior citizens compared how the city looks now contrasted with its past and explored how they

"Arts in the Millennium 2000"

Figure: 9.3. Arts in the Millennium 2000. (2000). Keepsake booklet, including artwork and photograph by Daniel Montano, Lois Walsh, and Ashley Taylor.

could illustrate both. This led to the creation of a performance piece integrating music, dance, and drama, and utilizing the work of local composers, arrangers, musicians, and songs written about the city. The exhibit included artwork of students and senior citizens and their visual interpretation of how the community has changed in the last 60 to 100 years. The writings also reflected this change.

Pittsburgh Neighborhoods, People and Cultures (see Figure 9.2). Pittsburgh's diverse ethnic neighborhoods and cultural traditions were explored in this theme

"Americana:
What it means to be an American"

Figure: 9.4. Americana: What it means to be an American. (2001). Keepsake booklet, including photographs by Emily Kellen, Aaron Cassandro, and Terrance Walters.

through ethnic music and dance performances reflecting the various cultures within the city. Some examples of the music and dances performed were the tarantella, riverdance, habañera, African and Jewish folk dances. The writings, photographs, and artwork reflected the various cultures found in each community utilizing their symbols and patterns in each composition.

Arts in the Millennium 2000 (see Figure 9.3). As a springboard for this theme, students, staff, and senior citizens viewed the "Carnegie International 1999/2000" exhibit at the Carnegie Museum of Art and focused on what the arts would be like in the new millennium. Participants decided on a title for the performance, the "Y-2 Kafe," a futuristic café where dancers and musicians performed. During the show, the audience was instructed to refrain from applauding and to merely respond by saying, "yum, yum, yum, yum" to the audiences delight.

For the exhibit, students and senior citizens represented what they thought art would look like in the future, using various combinations of mediums and "futuristic" techniques. During the performance, some of the artwork was projected onto the back wall of the stage along with some of the poetry written by the creative writing students. Besides being an intergenerational project, it also reinforces interdisciplinary ties and cooperation.

Americana: What it means to be an American (see Figure 9.4). Discussions were held between students and senior citizens while they attempted to answer this question. Each person's final response was unique. The art and media students focused on such things as American food, money, hobbies, and sports. They also included American symbols such as the flag, the Statue of Liberty, and the bald eagle. The performance included American folk songs and music such as George M. Cohen's "Yankee Doodle Dandy," as well as festive square dancing and Appalachian clogging.

Heroes, Art, and Culture (see Figure 9.5). Following the national tragedy that occurred on September 11, 2001, it seemed appropriate to reflect on what makes a person a hero. Students and senior citizens focused on those people in their lives whom they see as their heroes. The exhibit showcased works of art by students and senior citizens with their heroes, such as policemen, firemen, soldiers, parents, politicians, religious figures, and sports heroes. The creative writing students shared stories of their heroes and gave examples of their heroic deeds. The performance contained music and dance selections from composers and choreographers considered to be heroes in the field. Some of the music performed was "The Wind Beneath My Wings" by Larry Henley & Jeff Silbar, "When Johnny Comes Marching Home" by Roy Harris, and "Hero" by Mariah Carey & Walter Afanasieff. The dancers focused on dances from Balanchine and Fosse.

"Heroes, Art and Culture"
Exhibit and Performance

Figure: 9.5. Heroes, Art and Culture. (2002). Keepsake booklet, including artwork and photographs by Shan Womack, Rosemarie Druga, Justin Budd, and Ashlei McGivern.

Freedom (see Figure 9.6). Students and senior citizens focused on the word "freedom," discussing what it was and what it meant to each of them. They questioned where individual freedoms originated, what freedoms they currently enjoyed, and the people who were instrumental in securing those freedoms for us in this country. The exhibit included artwork of the Declaration of Independence, the Constitution, the American flag, Martin Luther King, Jr., George Washington, Abraham Lincoln, and women of the suffragette movement. Media students took photographs of things that meant "freedom" to them like skateboarding, listening to music, playing sports, and praying. Other participants developed a performance based on their reflections on "freedom" including several readings from the creative writing students and senior citizens, along with patriotic music and dance selections.

"Freedom"

Figure: 9.6. Freedom. (2003). Keepsake booklet, including artwork and photographs by Willa Jeffries and Sara Faigen, Brandon Moorefield, and Christina Keeney.

Setting Up the Art Exhibit

Several students and senior citizens carefully laid out the artwork, creative writings, and photographs for the exhibit on panels. Following the art teacher's direction and guidance, they matched the various pieces and arranged them in the order they would be placed on display. Students and seniors clipped the work onto the wire panels provided, making sure to attach name tags to each piece. When they were finished, they stepped back and looked carefully over all of the panels, being sure each piece was hung just right.

Performance Rehearsals

The dance, vocal, and instrumental music departments worked closely with each other to create a performance that would be educational and entertaining, as well as run smoothly. Students and senior citizens researched a particular style of music, choreography, composition, or an ethnic/cultural tradition or history related to the theme. They rehearsed in small groups during their scheduled music and dance classes, to fine tune their segment of the performance. Three days before the performance, all groups convened at school to stage the show, and rehearsed the production for the first time. During the rehearsal, participants learned where they would stand on the stage, as well as where they would make their exits and entrances, and in what order. It was explained what each group would wear and who would be responsible for the costumes as well as any props that would be needed. The program was checked for any last minute changes, being sure that each name was included and spelled correctly before it was sent off to the printer.

The day before the performance, all participants traveled to the performance site for a full day of rehearsal in the new location. As one watched the final rehearsal and viewed the set-up of the art exhibit, one could see the excitement build.

Showtime

On the day of the performance and exhibit, participants arrived two hours before the show was scheduled to begin, to afford time for a last-minute rehearsal. The display of art, media, and creative writings were checked one final time, being sure nothing fell off the panels overnight. Participants in the performance were backstage calming each other before the program began. Students and parents distributed programs and keepsake booklets to the audience as they arrived and were seated. Using the microphone, we announced that the program would begin in two minutes and for everyone to take a seat. The director of the senior citizens' group and I welcomed the audience, and explained the performance that they were about to view. The performance began!

Following the enthusiastic applause of the grand finale, all participants were then introduced to the audience, including staff and sponsors. The audience and participants were invited to view the exciting exhibit of artwork, photographs, and creative writings done by students and senior citizens, as they partook in a well deserved reception of cookies, punch and coffee, which were provided by the school.

At this time senior citizens and students were seen hugging each other, while parents attempted to gather them close for photographs. They exchanged phone numbers and shed a few tears with new friends made during the creation of this special artistic endeavor. As one senior imparted to me, "These school collaborations for me are very therapeutic and almost essential to keep me motivated," while another said, "I just love those kids!" A student told me, "Since my involvement in this project, I've become more familiar with the senior generation. Listening to their stories has opened up a whole new world for me." The magic that had transpired through the rehearsals, performance, and exhibit was evident. The generation gap had successfully and artistically been bridged.

10

Mel Alexenberg
and
Miriam Benjamin

Legacy Thrones: Intergenerational Collaboration In Creating Multicultural Public Art

The creation of "Legacy Thrones" is an exemplary model of intergenerational collaboration and postmodern art education. Elders representing different ethnic communities, high school and college art students, and artists collaborated in creating monumental works of public art that enriched their shared environment. Through aesthetic dialogue between young people and elders from the Hispanic, African-American, and Jewish communities of Miami, valued traditions of the past were transformed into artistic statements of enduring significance. Together, young and old hands shaped wet clay into colorful ceramic relief elements collaged onto three towering thrones constructed from steel, aluminum, and concrete. Installed in a park facing Biscayne Bay, each 20-foot high, 2-ton throne visually conveys the stories of the three largest ethnic communities of elders that had settled in Miami.

Creating public art through intergenerational collaboration enriched the lives of young people while adding vitality to the lives of elders. The more extensive life experience and wisdom of the elder offers a young person a sense of historical continuity and tried responses to the perennial questions of human existence unfold. At the same time, the young person, having more vitality, rejuvenates and invigorates the elder with energy and an influx of fresh ideas. "Without this exchange, the elder may remain locked in the past. With their penchant for experimentation and their forward-looking mentality, young people give elders the gist of encountering the present and anticipating the future" (Schachter-Shalomi & Miller, 1995, p. 192).

The benefits of intergenerational experiences have been supported by numerous researchers. The eminent psychologist Erik Erikson (1986) emphasized: "For the aging, participation in expressions of artistic form can be a welcome source of vital involvement and exhilaration. . . . When young people are also involved, the change in the mood of elders can be unmistakably vitalizing" (p. 318). Medical doctor and researcher Gene Cohen (2000), director of the Center on Aging, Health & Humanities at George Washington University and former president of the Gerontological Society of America, writes in the section "Intergenerational Collaborative Creativity: The Best of Both Worlds" in *The Creative Age*: "As we age, enormous potential lies in collaborative endeavors, especially of an *intergenerational* nature that brings the energy, experience, and vision of different ages together for problem solving or pure enjoyment" (p. 33).

Participatory Art

The Legacy Thrones project began as a dialog between two artists (the authors of this chapter) and representatives of the downtown Miami community. We worked closely with Ana Gelabert Sanchez, who at the start of the project directed the Neighborhood Enhancement Team for downtown Miami and later became the Director of Planning for the entire city. The project was funded by a federal grant to the City of Miami administered by the Downtown Development Authority. It was part of the revitalization of a rundown part of the city that included the redevelopment of Margaret Pace Park facing the bay and the building of Miami's Performing Arts Center designed by the renowned architect Cesar Pelli.

Through our dialog with people who lived, worked, and owned businesses in the downtown area it became clear that they desired a work of public art that honored different ethnic communities of Miami and invited their direct partici-pation in creating the artwork. We conceived of the idea of a magnificent throne as a metaphor for bestowing honor and explored throne designs with college art students from New World School of the Arts[1] in their course in environmental public art. Elders from the three largest ethnic communities of Miami were invited to join with these students in creating three thrones. African-American elders from the Greater Bethel AME Church, Hispanic elders from Southwest Social Services Program, and Jewish elders from the Miami Jewish Home for the Aged came to the New World School of the Arts to collaborate with art students of even broader cultural diversity in creating the three Legacy Thrones. College art students collaborated with the elders in the first phases of the project and were joined later by high school students.

We made presentations about the throne project to African-American elders at a church, to Hispanic elders at a senior center, and to Jewish elders at a home for the aged. Twenty women between ages 70 and 85 volunteered to participate in this intergenerational art project. No men volunteered. We explained that this program exemplified a new paradigm based on the notion of *participation* in which art would begin to redefine itself in terms of social relatedness. Legacy Thrones represents "the emergence of a more participatory, socially interactive framework for art . . . supporting the transition from the art-for-art's-sake assumptions of late modernism" (Gablik, 1991, p. 7).

In the process of planning how to gather historical and cultural information from the elders, we discovered Perlstein's (n.d.) methods of life review at Elders Share the Arts (ESTA) in New York City. Perlstein founded an arts organization that facilitated elders looking back and reaching inward to trigger reminiscences of events and images of personal and communal significance. She pioneered the use of life review as a creative tool for working with elders in intergenerational groups. We flew to New York to meet with Perlstein and learn about her innovative use of life review as it applied to intergenerational performance art. Subsequently, a grant from the National Endowment for the Arts enabled us to invite Perlstein to Miami to work with the elders and students at the beginning of the Legacy Thrones project.

Perlstein first met with the art students to expose their stereotyped views about older adults and to teach them ways to illustrate reminiscences from dialogues with their elder partners. She taught them how to develop and ask "questions to mine the riches of a person's stories" (Perlstein & Bliss, 1994, p. 27). At the first meeting with students and elders together, she used a number of exercises to encourage each elder to begin telling about her life experiences and cultural roots. She invited all the participants to look at their hands, to examine them in detail, touch them, place one hand on another, and feel them fully. As this hand meditation was going on, she suggested that they consider what their hands have done, where they have been, what journeys they had taken. Focusing on their hands triggered memories of things that the elders had done in long eventful lives. This tactile experience was particularly relevant since they would work with their hands in transforming memories into relief ceramic sculptures. A second exercise suggested that the elders look at their clothing or the clothing of their youthful partners and choose a color that they especially liked. Looking at a particular color was a powerful stimulus to memory and creative thought.

After the initial meeting with Perlstein, the elders continued to communicate their life experiences to the young people at each weekly session. At the second stage, three groups of elders arrived at New World School of the Arts, and were greeted by the students who escorted them into the studio for coffee and cake. We worked with the students and elders to facilitate the transformation of their reminiscences into visual/tactile images that could be expressed through clay.

The art students, experienced and skilled in ceramics, technically helped the elders work with clay to make relief sculptural statements of images from their personal and collective past. A Jewish woman who was a dancer in her youth with the Bolshoi Ballet in Moscow formed images of women dancing the horah, a traditional Jewish folkdance. An African-American woman made a mule-drawn wagon such as the one on which she rode to church as a child in rural Florida. A Cuban woman made high-heeled shoes and an elegant pocketbook, symbolizing the only valued possessions she took with her while escaping on a rickety boat that sailed across the Florida straits. Although most of the elders had no prior experience in art production or working with clay, their technical prowess and aesthetic judgment developed over a year of participation. They grew in self-confidence as they learned more about art and aesthetics and developed their skills working with clay. Critiques of their own artworks and those of other elders became more sophisticated as their art vocabulary grew.

Expressing Cultural Values

Complimenting their personal images, the elders made symbolic representations of communal experiences and shared cultural values. Jewish elders formed Hebrew letters, a Hanukkah menorah, the Biblical dove of peace, and symbols of the ten sephirot representing the stages in the parallel processes of human creativity and divine creation. African-Americans elders created images of Black slaves in agony, cotton fields of the rural South, the keyboard of their church's organ, African masks, and African geometric motifs. Hispanic elders made a guitar and maracas, a cup of Cuban coffee, baseball players, fighting cocks, an Aztec bird, a rainforest frog, Jesus with outstretched arms, and Mary with a sunburst halo. The elders' creations supported the postmodern definition of art as "a form of cultural production whose point and purpose is to construct symbols of shared reality" and the value of art as promoting "deeper understandings of the social and cultural landscape" (Efland, Freedman, & Stuhr, 1996, p. 72).

Figure: 10.1. Hispanic Throne. *Figure: 10.2.* Jewish Throne.

During the next phase, both young and older participants applied colorful glazes to the fired clay that would withstand the harsh environment facing the bay. These relief ceramic montage/pastiche forms became a collage cemented to the thrones until the sculptural surfaces were entirely clad in ceramics, a typical postmodern integration of art media (Efland, Freedman, & Stuhr, 1996), where "appropriation, collage, and juxtaposition of meanings are in" (Clark, 1996, p. 2). A mosaic of broken tiles filled the spaces between the collaged ceramic elements made by the elders and students. On the Jewish throne, hundreds of ceramic Hebrew letters where randomly arranged in the spaces between the relief ceramic sculptures. The letters where cut from clay and glazed and fired by the students. The elders did not participate in cementing the ceramics to the thrones. It was physically demanding and time consuming work. Different high school and college art students completed one throne at a time over a period of five years.

119

All three thrones were made the same size and basic shape to represent the equal status of the cultures. However, the form of each throne's crown and sides varied symbolically to express cultural uniqueness. The Hispanic throne has a sunburst crown and water waves cascading down the two sides (see Figure 10.1). The Jewish throne is topped by a Hanukkah menorah that holds nine flaming torches with an aluminum enlargement of leather straps meandering down the sides from a box containing scriptural passages worn by Jews on their heads during morning prayers (see Figure 10.2). On the head of the African-American throne is a huge African mask with its sides designed with a geometric pattern derived from a composite African motif (see Figure 10.3). The framework for each of the three thrones was constructed by welding steel pipes connected to each other with rebar rods to reinforce the concrete that filled the spaces between the pipes. One of the art students was a professional metal worker from Ecuador who supervised the other students in the construction of the thrones.[2] In order to move them, wheels where welded onto the two-ton thrones resting horizontally on the studio floor at the New World School of the Arts.

The students laid out the relief ceramic elements on the throne and experimented with arranging them in different relationships. The elders discussed the placement of the sculptures with each other, the students, and the principal artists. After the front and sides of the two ton thrones where fully clad in ceramics, they were transported to Margaret Pace Park for installation with a large tow truck and lifted up by a crane situating them in their permanent site on the shore of Biscayne Bay. The supporting steel pipes inside each throne protruding

Figure: 10.3. African-American Throne.

from under the throne seat were deeply imbedded in a concrete underground base. The thrones were designed to be strong enough to withstand Florida's hurricanes. After being installed, the wheels were cut off and the unfinished rear sides of the throne backs became accessible. Two of the students who had worked on the thrones when they rested horizontally in the studio, completed the rear on site after the thrones stood erect. They designed the backs to incorporate the remaining sculptures that had been made by the Hispanic and African-American elders. Decorative Hebrew letters for the rear of the Jewish throne were made by art students at Emunah College in Jerusalem and shipped to Miami. Ceramic elements made by Jewish elders in Miami collaged together with those made in the Land of Israel forges a powerful link with the elders' ancestral homeland.

Each throne honors the integrity of a monoculture rather than a multicultural mix. Harold Pearse (1997) suggests, "in the future, what was heralded as multiculturalism will give way to polyculturalism" (p. 37). Instead of being an expression of the outdated American concept of a "monotone meltdown pot," the thrones are more like vegetables in a salad, each retaining its own form and flavor. "This model is fresher and healthier; the colors varied; the taste often unfamiliar" (Lippard, 1990, p. 5).

> In a complex society such as ours which wishes to allow group differences to "emerge," not "submerge," we need to find ways for these groups to express themselves and be heard and valued. One of the major purposes of participation is to allow diversity to be expressed. (Halprin & Burns, 1974, p. 11)

While the elders were working on their separate thrones, not only did they learn to appreciate their differences, they also realized how much they shared. They recognized a dynamic balance between diversity and unity.

An example of postmodern art education, as evidenced in the Legacy Thrones, is based upon personal and emotional metaphors and the acknowledgment of the importance of narrative and personal myth (Jones, 1997). "Art is once again about something beyond itself; it defines a particular narrative or world view" (Anderson, 1997, p. 71). It is based upon collecting "little narratives," each presenting an alternative way of experiencing the world, "to show that each cultural story is but one among many" (Efland, Freedman, & Stuhr, 1996, p. 96).

Shared Values

In *Mixed Blessings: New Art in a Multicultural America*, Lucy Lippard (1990) praises "an intercultural art that combines a pride in roots with an explorer's view of the world as shared by others" and in "cultural dissimilarities and the light they shed on fundamental human similarities" (p. 4). Working parallel to each other in one large studio, the three culturally and ethnically different groups of elders continually engaged in dialogue with each other, an opportunity that rarely exists outside of the studio. African-American, Hispanic, and Jewish elders in their ethnically specific homes for the aged and senior centers seldom encounter each other. Working together and learning about each other's cultures, they came to realize how much they shared in experiences and in values. The theme of the Legacy Thrones art project became "Behold, how good and how pleasant it is when we sit together" (Psalm 133).

All three groups of elders shared their commitments to living in freedom and to Biblical values. Freedom from slavery and from the tyrannical regimes of Hitler and Castro shaped their reminiscences. Some women had heard first-hand stories of slavery on Southern plantations from their grandmothers. One Holocaust survivor spoke about having to bite the umbilical cord of her child born in hiding in an underground pit. Cuban exiles talked about escaping the brutal oppression on the island they loved.

Although the African-Americans were Protestant Christians, the Hispanics, Catholics, and the

Figure: 10.4. Details of the African-American Throne.

Jews, Jewish, they all shared appreciation for the freedom in America that germinated from common values found in the Hebrew Bible (referred to as the Old Testament by Christians) and expressed in the words inscribed on the Liberty Bell in Philadelphia: "Proclaim liberty throughout all the land unto all the inhabitants thereof" (Leviticus 25:10). The sculpted clay images showed their common appreciation for religious text. A sculptured book with the relief words "Holy Bible" grace the African-American throne (see Figure 10.4). Embellished Hebrew ceramic letters from a Biblical verse were made by

Figure: 10.5. Details of the Jewish Throne.

art students from Emunah College in Jerusalem to grace the Jewish throne (see Figure 10.5). And biblical figures shaped in clay create a spiritual presence on the Hispanic throne (see Figure 10.6). In reading the Biblical book of Exodus honored by both Jews and Christians, they learned about the Israelites escaping to freedom from Egyptian bondage as a universal symbol for the triumph of liberty over slavery. This symbol informed the thoughts of America's founding fathers. On July 4, 1776, the Continental Congress formed a high-powered committee, made up of Thomas Jefferson, Benjamin Franklin, and John Adams, to propose a seal and motto for the newly independent United States of America. They proposed a seal depicting the Israelites escaping to freedom from bondage under Pharaoh through the divided waters of the Red Sea, with Moses standing

Figure: 10.6. Details of the Hispanic Throne.

on the shore extending his hand over the sea while the waters overwhelmed the Egyptians with the motto: "Rebellion to Tyrants is Obedience to God" (Boyd, 1950).

We learn about the intimate connection between freedom of expression and artistic creation from the original Hebrew in the Exodus narrative. The prototypic artist-teacher is named the grandson of freedom. If we literally translate the full names of Bezalel and Oholiav, the principal artists in the collective creation of the Tabernacle in the desert, we see the modern sensibility of relating art to individual passion and free expression coupled with the postmodern collaborative enterprise of constructing a symbolic structure of an intergenerational reality shared by the entire community. *Bezalel ben Uri ben Hur* means "In the Divine Shadow son of Fiery Light son of Freedom." *Oholiav ben Akhisamach* means "My Tent of Reliance on Father, Son, and My Brother." The symbolism on the throne connects with past and future generations. Bezalel's name represents the psychology of the creative artist and Oholiav's name describes the sociology of collective creativity in a mutigenerational community. In *The Third Hand: Collaboration in Art from Conceptualism to Postmodernism*, Green (2001) proposes "that collaboration was a crucial element in the transition from modernist to postmodernism art and that the trajectory consisting of a series of artistic collaboration emerges clearly from the late 1960s conceptualism onward" (p. x).

Artist as Teacher

Ron Neperud (1995) writes in his introduction to *Context, Content, and Community in Art Education: Beyond Postmodernism,*

> Art in the postmodern sense is treated as not separate from the world, but as a vital part of human existence. Postmodernism demands that the audience of art become involved in the discursive process of discerning meaning. This postmodernist view of art means a very different approach to teaching about art (p. 5).

In the Bible, the roles of artist and teacher are integrated functions. The artists Bezalel and Oholiav are also gifted with the "ability to teach" (Exodus 35:34). As artist-teachers, they channel passion and freedom into nurturing the collaboration of young and old in creating a shared environment of spiritual power. Their roles as artists were to teach others to play their unique parts in a collaborative artistic creation, like players of different instruments working together to bring into being a great symphony. One of the most venerated religious thinkers of the twentieth century, J. B. Soloveitchik (1983), proposes that the dream of creation is *the* central idea in Biblical consciousness—"the idea of the importance of man as a partner of the Almighty in the act of creation, man as creator . . . a man who longs to create, to bring into being something new, something original" (p. 99). This longing for creation and the renewal of the cosmos is embodied in all of its goals.

Participatory art changes the visual artist's role to be more like a creative leadership role in the performing arts and education. Instead of a solitary role alone in one's studio, the postmodern paradigm finds the visual artist acting more like a choreographer in dance, composer/conductor in music, playwright/producer/director in theater and film, and a teacher/mentor in education. In the Legacy Throne art project, the two principal artists facilitated the collaboration of the young people and elders in Miami's multicultural community in playing roles like those of dancers, musicians, actors, and art students. Other faculty members, administrators, high school and college students at New World School of the Arts[3] and college students at Emunah College of Art[4] in Jerusalem also became involved in different stages of the process of creating the thrones from its beginnings to its final installation at its permanent site six years later.

Benefits of Lifelong Creativity

In our initial discussions with the activity directors of the senior centers about the participation of elders, they suggested that two elders be teamed up with each student. They were of the opinion that the elders would not be able to participate regularly because of health problems—being too tired, not feeling well enough to go out for the day, or having to visit a doctor. Dr. Sandra Walsh, Director of Research at University of Miami School of Nursing, was invited to use the thrones project for a pilot study of how participating in creative activities influenced their health. Four of her graduate research students became participant observers in the project. They worked as part of the creative teams of art students and elders interviewing the elders about their attitudes towards working on the thrones, recording their attendance, and discussing the reasons for their absences. Video artist Shelly Gefter documented the interviews and the process of interaction between the elders and the art students, their verbal dialog with each other, and their creative encounter with clay and glazes. In fact, the elders were rarely absent. One woman who required surgery for cancer, was back at work on the project in two weeks.

Dr. Walsh and her students found that the enthusiasm for participating in the creation of a monumental work of public art had a profound effect not only on the elders' mental health but also on their physical well-being. Their pilot study confirmed the hypothesis presented by Dr. Gene Cohen (2000):

> Experimental studies indicate that creative activities and their consequent positive effect on mood and morale can lead to an increased production of protective immune cells. We don't know why this is so. Perhaps, in the same way that sustained stress appears to lead to insidious, then serious problems with overall health, the sustained experience of the positive, health-affirming nature of the creative process delivers a heightened, satisfying, positive health effect. (pp. 61-62)

From High Touch to High Tech

The last day together was celebrated with a party in which the elders brought their different ethnic foods. We exhibited large photographs of the elders and students working on the Legacy Thrones. These photographs stimulated a lively discussion and insightful evaluation between elders and students. At a ceremony at the end of the day, we presented each of the elders with an elegant certificate of participation printed with her name. Each elder was honored and applauded. The photographs of the creation of the thrones were framed and exhibited in branches of Citibank in Miami.

Their joy turned sour when they realized that their weekly creative activity had come to an end. They insisted that we find a new project for them so they could return to the New World School of the Arts next year. The following year, we developed a Legacy Scrolls project for the same elders. In contrast to the high touch Legacy Throne project that told the collective story of each ethnic group, the high tech Legacy Scrolls told the life stories of each individual elder. Each elder brought images that told about them—family photographs, diplomas, newspaper clippings, embroidery, treasured objects, etc. These documents and objects were digitized and became the elements for creating a composite collage using Photoshop. Initially, the computer graphics students did the work as the elders sat by their side in front of the monitor. The elders soon became impatient and encouraged the students to teach them Photoshop so that they could actively participate in making the collages. The final collages were printed out in full-color on rolls of canvas. Each 3 x 20 feet Legacy Scroll honored an individual elder. Intergenerational collaboration in creating both Legacy Thrones and Legacy Scrolls is an expression of contemporary culture's way of balancing high tech and high touch experiences (Naisbitt, 2001).

References

Anderson, T. (1997). Toward a postmodern approach to art education. In J. Hutchens & M. Suggs (Eds.), *Art Education: Content and Practices in a Postmodern Era* (pp. 62-73). Reston, VA: National Art Education Association.

Boyd, J. (1950). *The papers of Thomas Jefferson,* (Volume I). Princeton: Princeton University Press.

Clark, R. (1996). *Art education: Issues in postmodern pedagogy.* Reston, VA: National Art Education Association.

Cohen, G. D. (2000). *The creative age.* New York: Avon Books.

Efland, A., Freedman, K., & Stuhr, P. (1996). *Postmodern art education: An approach to curriculum.* Reston, VA: National Art Education Association.

Erikson, E. H., Erikson, J. M., & Kivnik, H. Q. (1986). *Vital involvement in old age.* New York and London: Norton.

Gablik, S. (1991). *The reenchantment of art.* New York and London: Thames and Hudson.

Green, C. (2001). *The third hand: Collaboration in art from conceptualism to postmodernism.* Minneapolis: University of Minnesota Press.

Halprin, L., & Burns, J. (1974). *Taking part: A workshop approach to collective creativity.* Cambridge, MA: The MIT Press.

Jones, R. L., Jr. (1997). Modern and postmodern: Questioning contemporary pedagogy in the visual arts. In J. Hutchens & M. Suggs (Eds.), *Art education: Content and practices in a postmodern era* (pp. 91-102). Reston, VA: National Art Education Association.

Lippard, L. R. (1990). *Mixed blessings: New art in a multicultural America.* New York: Pantheon.

Naisbitt, J. (2001). *High tech high touch: Technology and our accelerated search for meaning.* London: Nicholas Brealey.

Neperud, R. W. (1995). *Context, content, and community in art education: Beyond postmodernism.* New York: Teachers College Press.

Pearse, H. (1997). Doing otherwise: Art education praxis in a postparadigmatic world. In J. Hutchens & M. Suggs (Eds.), *Art education: Content and practices in a postmodern era.* (pp. 31-39). Reston, VA: National Art Education Association.

Perlstein, S., & Bliss, J. (1994). *Generating community: Intergenerational partnership through the expressive arts.* New York: Elders Share the Arts.

Perlstein, S., Charnow, S., & Nash, E. (n.d.). *Life review training manual.* New York: Elders Share the Arts.

Schachter-Shalomi, Z., & Miller, R. S. (1995). *From age-ing to sage-ing.* New York: Warner Books.

Soloveitchik, J. B. (1983). *Halakhic Man.* Philadelphia: Jewish Publication Society of America.

Endnotes

[1] New World School of the Arts in Miami is a joint venture of Miami-Dade Public Schools, Miami-Dade College, and the University of Florida. It has four-year high school programs and B.F.A. and B.M. degree programs in the visual arts, dance, theater, and music. NWSA is the first art school in U.S.A. to offer a B.F.A. degree with a major in Environmental Public Art. Louise Romeo, current Dean of Visual Arts at New World School of the Arts was involved with the project from the beginning and played a central role in the last phases of making and installing the thrones when Mel Alexenberg and Miriam Benjamin had left Miami to live and work in Israel. NWSA art faculty Aramis O'Reilly, Robert Saxby, Susan Banks, and Wendy Wischer also participated in the throne project at different stages. Professor Anthony Ferdanez photographed the thrones.

[2] Victor Arias, NWSA student and professional metalworker, supervised work with steel, aluminum, and concrete in making the three thrones. Michele Ariemma, Gary Forseca, Miguel Luciano, and Jody Lyn-Kee-Chow were NWSA students who played major roles in creating the thrones.

[3] During their 10 years in Miami, Mel Alexenberg (Ed.D., art education, New York University) was Dean of Visual Arts at New World School of the Arts. Miriam Benjamin (M.F.A. ceramic sculpture, Pratt Institute) was Director of Intergenerational ArtLinks. Alexenberg's artwork is in the collections of more than 50 museums worldwide.

[4] Emunah College director, Amos Safrai, and sculpture instructor, Eva Avidar, were instrumental in facilitating the participation of Israeli art students in the throne project.

11

Diane B. Barret

Generations Together

This chapter describes three intergenerational art programs that took place in the Northeast Georgia area over the past seven years. Each program was designed to bring older adults into contact with young people in their communities, letting them share perspectives through art. The Grassroots Arts Program of the Georgia State Legislature provided funding for the projects, which were sponsored by local senior centers. In each case a classroom teacher recognized the value of intergenerational sharing and worked with senior center staff to coordinate scheduling and transportation for students and elders. The rewards of these efforts were obvious not only in the art that resulted but also in the continuing associations that evolved.

Background

While working toward an Ed.D. in art education at the University of Georgia in the early 1990s, I interned with a team of educators and students whose job was to design thematic programming for older adults in the arts and physical fitness. Classes were implemented at senior centers on a weekly basis, giving me regular exposure to elders and life in the centers. I quickly recognized the need for professionalism in developing visual arts classes for senior adults and became aware of their potential to be expressive and creative. My goal was to design programs that would tap into the humor, wisdom, and life experience evident among this group. Art could become a window into the world of a generation whose voice is often unheard.

It is not surprising that I soon became interested in developing intergenerational projects. I wanted to get older adults into meaningful dialogue with young people in their communities, letting them share perspectives through art. The Grassroots Arts Program of the Georgia State Legislature was a valuable funding resource for me. Over the next 12 years, I directed eight Grassroots Arts projects that brought generations together. While each project involved different media, all focused on a theme that was of interest to young and old. I will describe three of the most successful of these programs: (a) a photography project in Madison, Georgia, in which students and elders reflected on the question "What places in your community are important to you?;" (b) a history quilt project in Elberton, Georgia, which tapped into the memory of senior adults and the enthusiasm of young people as they researched the background of old photographs; and (c) a book arts program in Lexington, Georgia, which provided an opportunity for middle-schoolers to get to know senior adults through writing and interviews. In each case, a senior center director and a classroom teacher recognized the value of intergenerational sharing and were willing to make the extra effort to bring the groups together. The resulting programs created meaningful dialogue and, in some cases, on-going connections between young and old.

Celebrating Community

Madison, Georgia, is a small town of 3,500 people located about 60 miles east of Atlanta. It is noted for a remarkable number of antebellum homes that survived Sherman's march through the state during the Civil War. While driving to the Morgan County Senior Center, I passed those lovely, white-columned mansions and felt transported back in time to a much mythologized era of graciousness and beauty. Older adults at the center were very aware of community history and spoke with pride of their town and its dedication to preserving historic homes and buildings. They were, for the most part, retired blue-collar workers or housewives living on modest incomes. The senior center was an important part of their lives because it provided transportation, hot lunches, health-promotion programs, and enriching educational experiences.

Planning the Project

A conversation with senior center staff in the fall of 1996 led to the idea of writing a Grassroots Arts grant proposal for an intergenerational photography project to take place the following spring. The director was eager to find ways of connecting elders at the center with young people. Using photography as a medium would provide many older adults who did not own cameras with their first opportunity to take photographs. The choice of "Celebrating Community" as a theme would tap into an area in which the elders were already keenly interested and also would be a potentially fascinating focus for students. The next step was to find a teacher interested in working with us.

The principal of the local elementary school suggested Connie Shumake, a special-education teacher whom he thought would be "the perfect person for you to work with." I met with Connie the following week. Her enthusiasm about the project was equal to mine. She, too, felt there needed to be more opportunities for young and old to come together and share thoughts and feelings. She added her own ideas about expanding activities for students to include computer-generated narratives that would accompany the photos. This made the activity tie in with the writing curriculum for first through fourth grades. As we brainstormed about ways to bring the groups together, we discovered that it would be impossible to do more than have a joint reception for the photographers at the end of the project. Because Connie was the special-education instructor, her time with students was limited and on a strict schedule. Her classes were mainly in the afternoon, while my classes with older adults had to take place in the morning. Given these limitations, we agreed that I would come to the elementary school to present a motivational lecture and give instructions on using recyclable cameras. Connie would direct her students as they took photographs and wrote narratives, and the two of us would meet bi-weekly to discuss how the project was going.

Implementation of the Project

We were notified in January that we had received a grant and the project began the following April with an introductory lecture at the monthly AARP meeting held at the senior center. I showed slides of a special exhibition at the Georgia Museum of Art entitled "A Turn of the Century View of Athens." Photographs taken in the early 1900s of Athens, Georgia, and the surrounding area gave the 25 senior viewers a chance to discuss the ways communities have changed over their lifetime. Following the lecture, a van took 10 participants to Athens for a first-hand viewing of the photography exhibit.

The following week, 18 older adults attended a photography class at the senior center and set out to document their community using recyclable cameras. Their task was to capture places that were important to them—places that made Madison seem like home. At the same time, elementary students were presented with the theme and taught how to use their cameras. Because the budget was limited and 35 students were involved, it was decided to let two students share one 27-exposure camera. Over a 2-week period, both groups photographed places in and around Madison. After the film was developed, each person selected one image to be enlarged, matted, and framed for exhibition at the Madison Artist Guild in June. Participants also wrote narratives to accompany the photographs, explaining their meaning in further detail. While students typed their essays on computers, it was necessary to record the stories of senior adults who lacked writing skills. Others hand-wrote their narratives, and I transcribed all stories on computer using a format Connie and I had predetermined.

The matting of photographs and mounting of narratives for both groups fell to me as project director. It was interesting to see what young and old had chosen to photograph and to read their stories about the images. Students had approached the project with a freshness and honesty that made the work both humorous and endearing. Seniors had conveyed a sense of history and nostalgia in their photographs. A breakdown on subject matter yielded the following results from 35 elementary students: (a) five photographed their grandparent's home or garden, (b) seven photographed their own home, (c) eight chose something in nature (my tree, creek, lake, yard, etc.), (d) seven photographed their church, (e) three selected the Uncle Remus Library, (f) three chose historic buildings, (g) two photographed sports fields, and (h) two photographed their summer camp. Of the 16 older adults involved, (a) seven photographed their church as an important place (*our church has given us roots in the community and a place to serve*), (b) five chose something in nature (trees, gardens), (c) three photographed buildings that held memories and a sense of history (everything from a service station to the old Buckhead jail), and (d) one photographed her family cemetery.

The culminating event of the project was an exhibition of photographs entitled "Celebrating Community Through the Eyes of Children and Older Adults" displayed at the Madison Artist Guild from June 21 through July 12. A reception honoring young and old was held on Sunday, June 22, with over 90 people attending. It was an exciting event for both groups, who had been hearing about each other throughout the project but were meeting for the first time. Each senior photographer was partnered with two students to tour the exhibit. There was much animated dialogue as photographers explained their image and looked at what others had done. Some interesting connections surfaced during the party. One young person discovered that both he and his Sunday school teacher had chosen to photograph their church as an important place. There was also a grandmother-grandson duo who participated in the project. The grandson had photographed his great-grandmother's home where he and his parents still lived. His grandmother had photographed the Madison-Morgan Cultural Center, a local museum where she had once attended elementary school. It was obvious they shared and appreciated their deep roots in Madison (see Figure 11.1).

The local newspaper reviewed the show in this way:

> The thing that amazed and impressed us was the sensitivity the children had toward their subjects; there is a real reverence for what they hold special ....With the combined works, a visitor gains a highly appreciative sense of where the children and seniors are from, representing a reflective mosaic of Morgan County. Man-made and natural wonders are part of the landscape, and those are represented in "Celebrating Community." Beyond that observation is a deeper claim by each artist. It is a search for, and eventual discovery of, a safe haven. (Kelly, 1997)

Figure: 11.1. Harriette Wade and grandson Josh Stephens reveal their deep roots in Madison, Georgia, at a reception for the exhibition *Celebrating Community*. Josh photographed his three-generational family home. Harriette photographed the Madison Morgan Cultural Center where she attended school in the 1930s.

Discussion

While there were many positive aspects to this intergenerational project, its weakness seems obvious: there were few opportunities for young and old to come together to discuss ideas and share the entire process. The intergenerational component would have been greatly enhanced if the two groups could have met for the introductory class and at least one other time as they were taking photographs. This is something to work toward in future programming. The project did allow both young and old to express feelings and thoughts about what is important to their sense of community. It gave them new skills in using a camera. Both groups were given a positive exposure in the Madison area though the exhibition and newspaper article. Finally, the project reinforced areas of commonality between generations as they discovered a deep bond in their love of home and community.

A Community History Quilt Project

Located about 100 miles northeast of Atlanta, Elberton, Georgia, is known locally as *the granite capital of the world*. It boasts a long history of mining granite and manufacturing tombstones, which are then shipped across the United States. Over the last century, European artisans immigrated to Elberton to serve as carvers and sculptors, giving the city a mix of ethnic groups unusual in this part of Georgia. The Elbert County Senior Center serves a large number of older adults who are retired farmers, quarrymen, housewives, truck drivers, teachers, etc. Beginning in 1996, the center had received Grassroots Arts funding for a variety of projects, two of which included an intergenerational component. The director was always eager to write new proposals and determined to find the needed matching funds to make a project happen.

The Planning Stage

In the fall of 1998, the senior center staff and I sat down to brainstorm about a third intergenerational program. Building on the strong interest in quilting among older adults at the center, we concluded that it was an ideal setting for a community history quilt project. Many older adults at the center had lived in Elbert County since the early to mid-1900s and had a first-hand knowledge of how the community had grown and changed. Involving students in the project would give elders an opportunity to share their knowledge of local history as well as their quilting skills. Thus it was with great delight that the senior center received a 1999 Grassroots Arts grant to create a quilt that would document 100 years of Elbert County history.

I contacted Alice Terry, the special-education instructor at the Elbert County Middle School who had worked with me in the past, to see if her classes would be interested in the quilt project. Ms. Terry valued the time her students had spent with elders during previous projects, feeling they had greatly benefited from their intergenerational contact. A vibrant and energetic teacher, she immediately saw the value of this project as a lesson in community history as well as an opportunity for her students to learn more about the quilting process. During our brainstorming session it was decided that all of her students would attend an introductory lecture at the senior center to kick off the program. We would involve young people as much as possible throughout the project, bringing smaller groups to the center twice to help with the selection of images and the actual quilting. Her students would take on the tasks of researching the history behind old photographs and compiling a book about them. Then we would have a gathering of all participants in May to celebrate the completion of the quilt.

Implementation of the Project

Since the goal of the project was to create a quilt that would tell a story, we began in early February with a slide lecture at the center on the narrative quilts of Harriet Powers and Faith Ringgold. Twenty middle-school students were transported to the lecture in the senior center's vans. The students seemed very interested in learning more about quilting as they sat at tables and chatted with older participants. At this first meeting of young and old, several group decisions were made: (a) photo-transfer techniques would be used to print images to fabric, (b) fabrics would be selected that were similar to the gray-blue colors in Elberton granite, and (c) the quilt would be displayed in a downtown location accessible to the public.

The first four weeks of the project were devoted to gathering photographs that documented people and events in Elbert County from the early 1900s to the present. Alice Albertson, an active Senior Center Board member, accompanied me on photo-taking trips around the county. "The Elberton Star," the Elbert County Historical Society, the African-American Cultural Center, Elbert County High School, and seniors and staff all contributed images. Six students came to the senior center during one class to help select photos to be used in the quilt. Twenty photos were chosen, some black-and-white and some in color. One student suggested juxtaposing current images of Elberton and photographs of Elberton from the past in a single square. This enabled the group to utilize even more of the photographs. After transferring pictures to fabric squares, the quilt was pieced together at the senior center during the first week in April. At the same time middle-school students were researching the history behind each image, working on a book that would accompany and explain the quilt.

Quilting began in earnest in mid-April. A group of six students came to the center to help older adults pin the three quilt layers together. They were eager to learn more about the quilting process and added much enthusiasm to the event. Mrs. Kathlene Trippe, an experienced Elbert County quilter, contributed her expertise by doing the actual quilting. Moneys from the grant were earmarked for her work, thus meeting a grant goal of supporting local artists.
To celebrate the completion of the quilt at the end of April, the senior center hosted a party on Tuesday, May 4th. Students read from the book they had

Figure 11.2. The Elberton history quilt on display in the lobby of Regions Bank in downtown Elberton, Georgia.

compiled on the historical background of photographs used in the quilt. The teacher, Alice Terry, paired two students with each senior adult, so that they could question him or her about their memories and experiences of life in Elberton. The local newspaper came to take pictures and write an article about the quilt. Refreshments were served amid an atmosphere of excitement and satisfaction at the successful completion of a project that would be a contribution to the entire community (see Figure 11.2).

The history quilt was exhibited in the lobbies of two local banks during the following summer and fall. These highly visible public venues allowed many of Elbert County's citizens to view the quilt and to reminisce about the photographs. After that, the Senior Center Board decided to house the quilt at the center where it could be enjoyed by many for years to come. It still hangs there today and is something the seniors and staff point out with pride.

Discussion

Having an intergenerational focus greatly enhanced a project that could have been confined to the senior center alone. It brought elders and students together as they learned about African-American artists' use of quilts to convey personal and community history. Older adults became teachers as they led students through the entire process of making a quilt, from the design stage through assembly and quilting. Both groups shared perspectives and creative ideas with one another throughout the project. Young people brought a great deal of life and enthusiasm into the senior center when they came for classes and programs. They also added depth to the project through their historical research. Finally, both groups gained a true sense of accomplishment in creating a beautiful work of art that reflected pride in the city of Elberton. This history quilt project was not only about community, it created a sense of community among those who participated.

Sharing Our Stories: An Intergenerational Book Arts Project

When I headed up Highway 78 to Lexington, Georgia, one cold November day in 1997, I sensed that I was embarking on a wonderful adventure. The Oglethorpe County Senior Center had been awarded a small Grassroots Arts grant to fund a book project for ten of their older adults. They would be recording their life stories and designing book illustrations and covers. I had helped them write the grant and was looking forward to spending several weeks with elders who live in this rural part of Georgia.

Connecting the Senior Center and the Middle School

When we wrote the grant proposal, Senior Center Director Margaret Munday and I had decided to make this an intergenerational program. The center was located next door to the local middle school, and Ms. Munday could see the potential in facilitating a way for students and older adults to connect. I contacted the middle school's principal and was given the name of sixth-grade teacher, Anne Gillis, who would *probably be interested*. Indeed, she was. Her enthusiasm about letting her students mix and mingle with older adults generated some exciting ideas. Our brainstorming session resulted in a plan to cover a five-month period. We would invite a theater company from Kentucky that facilitated community oral-history projects to launch the program. The sixth graders would compile a book on local history while senior adults worked on their individual life stories. Finally, we would have a reception for both groups at the local library where the books could be shared and displayed.

Implementation of the Project

The opening event was exciting. On November 15, twelve older adults attended a performance of the Appalachian Roadside Theater in the middle-school gymnasium. Special seats had been allocated for the elders in front of bleachers which held the more than 100 sixth graders. Following the performance of storytelling and bluegrass music, students from Ms. Gillis's class and the group from the Senior Center went back to the classroom and participated in a workshop led by actors from the company. Groups of eight students conducted guided interviews with older adults, taping their responses to questions as well as their stories and reminiscences. The middle school had invited the elders to stay for lunch, and each older adult was accompanied and assisted by three students. This extra time was well spent, as rapport improved among the group members while they ate and chatted informally. A final meeting in the gymnasium with actors from the theater company was the culminating event of the day. Students were given the opportunity to share what they had learned from older adults and honor them for their wisdom, humor, and life experience. One of the seniors commented that students had "made us feel like kings and queens." It was obvious that the success of the day was due in part to careful planning and preparation by middle-school teachers and administrators who had encouraged student interest and sensitivity.

With this as motivation, older adults began a book arts class in January at the senior center to record significant memories and events from their lives. Their books contained photographs, drawings, collages, and narratives that reflected their genealogy and life history. Audio recordings were made of elders relating

Figure: 11.3. Teacher Anne Gillis shows older adults the book, *Just Us Folks*, that her students made about the history of Oglethorpe County at a reception for elders and sixth graders at the local library.

to their personal histories. These were then transcribed into computer files and printed on decorative paper. With the assistance of Frank Saggus, a local printmaker, the final hard-bound copies were covered in handmade paper and hand sewn.

Using additional Grassroots Arts funding, middle-school students in Anne Gillis' class were also involved in creating a book that spring. Working collectively, they contributed photographs of places in Oglethorpe County and stories they gathered from interviews with local residents. All of the text was computer-printed by the students. Ms. Gillis noted: "Every step of the process had to be done as a group, but they did it. It was the first time in years I have seen students work so cooperatively." Three copies of the book, entitled "Just Us Folks," were bound by the students and presented to the Senior Center, the local library, and the middle school.

In order to get the groups back together, middle-school students hosted a reception for the authors at the Oglethorpe County Library in April. The library was eager to display all of the books so that the public could enjoy these documents of personal and community history. Older adults were enormously proud of the books they had created and looked forward to sharing them with the students they had met the previous November. After everyone had arrived, students served refreshments to their older friends, and then both groups read selected stories (see Figure 11.3). The editor of the local newspaper, "The Oglethorpe Echo," covered the event, writing an excellent article that reinforced the importance of creating opportunities for dialogue between young and old.

Long-term Effects

Since this initial intergenerational project, connections between the senior center and the middle school have continued. Today sixth-grade students come monthly to read to older adults, which helps the students to improve their language skills in an atmosphere that is supportive and nonjudgmental. The visits include time for informal conversation and refreshments. Another middle-school alternative program called "Crossroads Kids" brings students to the senior center, where they implement special art projects at Valentine's Day, Easter, and Christmas. Senior center Director, Margaret Munday, is enthusiastic about the interaction older adults have with these extremely thoughtful and well-behaved young people. The "Sharing Our Stories" project initiated a long-term partnership and opened doors of continuing dialogue between generations.

Conclusion

The field of art education is only beginning to explore the area of intergenerational programming. The three projects described here can serve as models, each with its particular strengths and weaknesses. Selecting a theme that is interesting and meaningful to both age groups seems to be critical to the success of a project. In these cases, the focus on community provided a common area of interest and concern that was motivational for young and old. Hausman (1998) presents the challenge of providing meaningful programs for older adults that draw on the past in a way that illuminates the present. In all three projects, the memories and life experience of older participants were brought to bear as they photographed important places in the community, gathered photographs for a history quilt, and shared their life stories. Under the guidance of teachers who valued what older adults had to share, students learned from elders and experienced them as creative, contributing people. Students brought to the projects their own gifts of enthusiasm, energy, and fresh vision.

One of the difficulties in developing intergenerational programs is finding ways to bring groups together. Managing the logistics of transportation and class schedules requires a great deal of work. Often the demands of a jam-packed school day leave little or no room for an extra activity. Senior centers in rural areas of Georgia must plan programming between the hours of 10 a.m. and 12 p.m. so that older adults can have a hot lunch and be taken home before the middle of the afternoon. Given these parameters, the workable number of meetings between young and old is seldom ideal. Perhaps as more and more intergenerational programs occur, schools and senior centers will find better ways to facilitate them. Churches and community art centers are also gathering places for young and old that can provide more venues for intergenerational activities.

These three projects demonstrate that art can be a catalyst for creating a sense of community. As youth and elders come together, each group brings their own vantage point to the creative task. They often complement each other as wisdom encounters curiosity, life experience meets naiveté, and energy fuels reflection. In a culture that tends to separate older adults from the rest of the community, the field of art education has much to offer. We have the tools to open closed doors and to celebrate what each life-stage has to offer as we bring generations together.

References

Hausman, J. (1998). Thoughts about an intergenerational arts project. In D. Fitzner & M. Rugh (Eds.), *Crossroads: The challenge of lifelong learning* (pp. 72-78). Reston, VA: National Art Education Association.

Kelly, M. H. (1997, July 3). *Celebrating Community* presents a photographic essay on special places. *The Madisonian,* p. 6.

12

Alison Aune

Behind The Tomato Curtain: Interdisciplinary Museum-Based Learning

This chapter presents a descriptive example of an art education program conducted jointly by university faculty and museum staff. The aim of the program is to promote interdisciplinary learning among college age students and community children through exhibition-related art experiences in the museum. The program's distinctive features will be illustrated by an overview of five exhibitions and a discussion of the pedagogical methods used by students majoring in art education, elementary education, and early childhood education to develop critical engagement and artistic discovery in children through direct contact with original works of art.

Art Education: A Museum-Based Approach

For the past five years, Alison Aune and Jen Dietrich, members of the art education faculty of the Department of Art and Design, University of Minnesota,

141

Duluth, together with Peter Spooner and Susan Hudec, curator and education director, respectively, of the Tweed Museum of Art at the University, have been developing and implementing a new partnership in art education teacher training and community outreach. Their shared pedagogical and philosophical approach to art education combines traditional teaching strategies with experimental innovations associated with selected museum exhibitions. As a result, their program fosters possibilities that "expand the range of instructional practices" (Delacruz, 1997, p. 83) and broadens the domain of content knowledge in art. It promotes innovative inquiry, artistic creativity, and meaningful learning for the students and the children participating in it.

The exhibitions involved in the program feature works from the Tweed Museum's permanent collection as well as from traveling exhibitions and temporary guest exhibitions. These exhibitions include a wide variety of artworks ranging from historic to postmodern, international to regional, and traditional to conceptual, which represent an inclusive view of diverse styles, content, media, cultural traditions, and contemporary movements. The exhibitions provide unique educational opportunities for learners of all ages to become dynamically involved in investigations involving aesthetics, art criticism, and art history, and to confront a variety of issues related to visual culture, artistic diversity, and socially responsible engagement in the appreciation and production of art.

Overview of Coursework

Each semester, assignments in the education courses are modified and adjusted to integrate the featured museum exhibitions into the curriculum. Each exhibition is introduced to the preservice students as soon as it opens. For most education students not majoring in art education, this may be their first visit to an exhibition. The museum staff initially presents an introductory lecture and a gallery tour. They also provide informational handouts and make available research materials related to the exhibition. During the following weeks, students return to the museum at regular intervals to complete class assignments. These assignments include exercises in close observation, gallery drawing, formal critical analysis of artworks, museum based quizzes, and the creation of original instructional materials such as activity booklets, big museum books for children, museum games, and art projects that will be used in the museum by visiting school groups. The featured exhibition will also become the basis for the creation of individual studio projects and the development of lesson plans for the students' teaching portfolios.

All students will have opportunities during and outside of class to work with children as gallery teachers for museum tours, as participants in Saturday art classes for children, and as contributors to family day programs. As gallery teachers, the students will be assisted by museum staff in using a variety of instructional strategies to guide children through the exhibitions and to contribute positively to related art activities. This aspect of the course enables students to apply the learning theories and educational strategies they are studying. The museum environment offers an alternative setting for supervised preservice fieldwork. Here, the student begins the transition from student to teacher in an environment that encourages intergenerational teaching and learning. The challenge of motivating and promoting meaningful aesthetic experiences in many students not majoring in art is often substantially relieved when children enter the museum.

The museum tours generally begin in the lecture gallery. At this time museum staff greet the groups, introduces the college students, and present a brief slide overview to present "clues" on aspects of the featured exhibition. At the end of this introduction, small groups are formed of college students and children, and together they head out on their adventure as "art detectives." It is during this time that significant intergenerational learning occurs. Even though the students have already studied the exhibition by creating studio artworks, lesson plans, and instructional materials based on it, the gallery dialogue with children induces them to begin looking more deeply into the works and seeing the art in a new way. Because "children experience strong, open, and unmasked responses to art, they see with a sincerity and clarity that eludes an adult" (Waterfall & Grusin, 1991, p. 41). Our experience shows that many students become inspired by the children's enthusiastic responses to an exhibition. The children's imaginative responses and direct observations to original art enrich the college student's perceptions, and the student's enriched perceptions in turn enhance the child's experience in the class. The child and the student may thus work together, searching for aesthetic clues, engaging in critical discussions, participating in gallery drawing or other means of hands-on learning to discover new ways of seeing and understanding the world through art.

Specific Examples of Intergenerational/Interdisciplinary Learning in the Art Museum, 1999-2003

The following descriptive examples of five exhibitions contributed to interdisciplinary and intergenerational learning. These exhibitions exemplify the variety of styles, media, and inclusive content that is regularly featured as part of the exhibition schedule. Each exhibition is intended to make the museum "a facilitating environment," an alternative space for the exchange of creative ideas, interpretations, and discovery that "provoke imagination and critical reflection" (Burton, 2000, p. 343).

Figure 12.1. Tomato Curtain

Botanica: Looking behind the Tomato Curtain—A Discovery Approach

The exhibition entitled *Botanica: The Contemporary World of Plants* opened at the Tweed in 1999, before it moved to seven other institutions. Its curator, Peter Spooner, selected relevant works by 58 different artists. These works exemplified a wide variety of artistic styles ranging from still life paintings (reminiscent of 17th century Dutch) to contemporary visual experiments with tree drawings, mushroom prints, and the artistic documentation of plants used for bioremediation. The inherent interdisciplinary nature of the exhibition led to investigations into interesting connections between art and botany, art and biology, art and natural history, and environmental science.

Tomato Curtain (see Figure 12.1), done by the Minnesota artist Jean Humke in 1997-1998, was made from 2000 slices of dried tomatoes and pieced together with steel wire. It was hung as an indoor installation, a fact that evoked multi-sensory curiosity in students and children alike. For most, it was their first exposure to an installation piece, especially one made from tomatoes. The work demanded active participation on the part of the viewers. It seemed to invite investigation and speculation about its "meaning." The conceptual nature of the piece offered a venue for contemplation, humor, and sometimes poignant insights. As art detectives, the college students used questioning strategies to guide the group discussion. Questions such as "Why did the artist use tomatoes in her work? and "Is she an artist-farmer?" led to complex reflections. When a college student mentioned that the artist was inspired by her grandmother's garden and skills as a quilt maker, children began to find connections between the chores of canning or drying too many tomatoes and the way the tomatoes were stitched together like a quilt. This questioning technique fostered a cooperative approach to decoding the work to find meaning, to make a personal connection to what is being seen, and to develop an alternative understanding and possible appreciation, thus making a "fusion" between "a visual form and a conceptual artmaking strategy" (Gude, 2004, p. 8). In a small way, this discovery experience fosters a beginning aesthetic sensitivity to conceptual installation art.

First Nations Woodland Painting: Contextual Multicultural Approaches

In addition to the many in-depth exhibitions of traditional and contemporary Minnesota Ojibwe artworks arranged by staff at the Tweed Museum of Art, the *First Nations Woodland Painting* exhibition featured Canadian Ojibwe artists. The works included in this temporary exhibition comprised the Helen E. Band Collection of First Nations Art from the Thunder Bay Art Gallery. Their presence at the Tweed Museum during the fall semester of 2000 was the occasion for extensive interdisciplinary programming on art and culture for both college students and community children.

The *First Nations Woodland* exhibition included paintings by Norval Morrisseau, who was the innovator and founder of the Woodland style. He was the artist who in the 1960s began to study the ancient teachings of the sacred Midewewin birch-bark pictographic scroll paintings and to synthesize these teachings with modernist artistic styles and new media. "He felt that his work was related to the shaman's scrolls. . . . his Woodland paintings are characterized by images of nature, animals, and humans depicted in bold colors within flat, black outlined shapes, representing the stories and mythological characters which have long been a part of the spiritual world-view of Native Canadians" (Spooner, 2004, p. 26). Another featured artist in the exhibition was Roy

Thomas, who was deeply inspired by Morrisseau's work and the ancient Ojibwe pictographs. Thomas attended the exhibition and spoke to our students.

Figure: 12.2. First Nations Woodland

This exhibition was significant for the preservice students who would later take a required course called *Teaching American Indian Students* during their apprenticeships. The students were first given an extensive tour of the exhibition and then invited to hear Thomas speak about his work and its cultural context. He explained that he painted spiritually derived images to establish a connection to his ancestry and to keep his culture alive. He told the students that all aspects of an Ojibwe painting have symbolic importance for the Ojibwe. He spoke about the formal aspects of his brightly colored, linear x-ray styled paintings. Thomas's talk was important for understanding the sensitive nature of the indigenous Ojibwe culture and the relevance of that culture for the appreciation of their art. Students were concerned about the issue of respectful appropriation in their use of Woodland imagery for their own Ojibwe-inspired studio works, lesson plans, and instructional materials (see Figure 2). Thomas encouraged their active participation to keep a culture visible through art. He explained that "all the Elders of the world inspire us to paint the gift of sharing."

Art education students created several Woodland-inspired activity booklets for school groups. The information for the booklets was obtained from the Native American Resource Center on campus and included accurate and culturally sensitive information for children and youth about traditional Ojibwe spiritual beliefs, color symbolism, and stories about mythological creatures. The booklets also included vocabulary words, maps, and suggestions for Woodland-inspired art activities. When the art education students guided children through the exhibition, they were able to use their activity books as important teaching tools and as compositional frameworks to visually respond to the exhibition. The activity books also served as post-tour resources to reinforce the intergenerational museum experience and build cultural understanding.

Post-Hypnotic: **A Formalist Approach for Preschoolers**

In the spring semester of 2001, the Tweed Museum featured the traveling exhibition, *Post-Hypnotic*, which was assembled by Barry Blinderman of the University Galleries at Illinois State University. This visually dazzling Op Art exhibition became a major focus for the early childhood art education class. These students, none art-majors, were challenged to explore non-representational art in their own studio work and lesson-plan development. The culmination of this exploration would be a special 45-minute *Post-Hypnotic* program for preschoolers (ages 3-5) in the museum.

In preparation for the preschool program, the class was broken into four groups. Each group was given a theme: the Circles and Dots, the Squares, the Lines and Stripes, and the Plaids/Checkerboard groups. Their task was to create inquiry-based, hands-on activities appropriate for preschoolers that would encourage such children to explore the exhibit and identify the group themes (the Circles and Dots, and so on) exemplified there. Students were required to create original teaching materials for the program, to use only child- and museum-safe materials, and to use innovative teaching techniques. Each group created a Magic Box. This box was to be decorated with their group theme and to be filled with six museum activities related to that theme. The development of exhibition-specific instructional materials resulted in the creation of *Post-Hypnotic* name tags, Shape and Color activity booklets, big Op Art museum books for preschoolers, *Post-Hypnotic* pattern puzzles, Op Art matching games, and gallery props such as *Post-Hypnotic* "art detective" glasses and museum-floor shapes.

On the day of the program, students had pre-arranged their art stations, placing the Magic Boxes in an area for their group. The preschoolers were greeted by the college students dressed in theme-specific clothes, and were divided into groups before heading off into the galleries. Together, the groups explored the museum in search of their shapes, finding clues and solving puzzles in their activity booklets, before sitting down to open their Magic Box for expanded art projects (see Figure 12.3). One Magic Box activity that fostered a reciprocal intergenerational learning experience was the making of a collaborative collage. A variety of bold patterned wrapping paper was cut and torn into pieces. The students and children worked together to fit pieces together; finding composi-

Figure: 12.3. Post-Hypnotic

148

tional solutions together to create a new, optically charged, arrangement of shapes, colors, and abstract patterns. In this way, the artistic process of discovery was shared between the adult and child.

The students' playful approach to creating instructional materials was met with great joy by the younger participants. This art experience was an alternative and effective way to actively engage the college students with non-traditional preschool art forms; the innovative teaching resources that the students created and used in the museum provided high-quality, hands-on learning opportunities in art for preschoolers.

Made in Minnesota: **An Approach to Visual Culture**

In the spring semester of 2002, *Here By Design: Made in Minnesota* was a guest exhibition whose curators were James Boyd-Brent, Lindsay Shen, and Peter Spooner. In this exhibition, the process of critically seeing and closely examining the "multi-disciplinary nature of design" (Boyd-Brent and Shen, 2001, p. 3) and visual culture was central. The exhibition featured a wide variety of artifacts from regional sources, from traditional Minnesota Ojibwe baskets to contemporary skateboards, digital designs for advertising, comic books, silverware and kitchen utensils, outdoor wear, furniture, Scandinavian-style textiles, architectural models, and an actual small airplane. The exhibition provided students and children with the opportunity to discuss the design aspects of visual culture. It also opened a dialogue about the aesthetic realities and aesthetic possibilities of everyday objects in their lives.

For part of their exhibition-related coursework, students worked in small groups on a particular aspect of the exhibition to create design workbooks. The students were the gallery teachers for a number of K-12 school-group tours to the exhibit. Students and children visited the galleries together, discussing the works and designing in their workbooks their own product advertisements or their own logos for airplanes, cereal boxes, coats, or skateboards (see Figure 12.4). The directed discussion about these regional artifacts moved beyond the museum and Minnesota into the broader space of the environment in which the participants lived and heightened their awareness of the world around them in a positive way: It enhanced their ability to "critically negotiate a visually saturated world" (Gaudelius & Speirs, 2002, p. 15). As a result of the museum tours, the gallery observations, and the product designs, the discussions evolved into complex guided talks on art, popular culture, and mass media.

This *Made in Minnesota* exhibition was relevant to the interests of everyone participating in our program. The aesthetic dimensions of product design in the exhibition was related to the children's culture of cartoon designs on cereal

Figure: 12.4. *Made in Minnesota*

boxes, toothpaste, and socks, and the college student's culture of tattoos, CD covers, and designer jeans. The museum dialogue springing from the exhibit not only helped to sharpen the critical abilities and observational skills of the participants; it also increased their sensitivity to the visual features of the world around them.

To encourage playfulness in relation to great works of art prepares the way for teaching children to be free in critiquing it, exploring the ways in which art reflects and re-inscribes not only the positive aspects of culture, but also the negative, unjust, and limiting aspects of the culture (Sipe, 2001, p. 209).

This initial outcome of sharpened critical abilities and observational skills should produce a new way of looking at the aesthetic possibilities of everyday objects and product design, and also plant the seeds for informed critical thinking about visual culture. The intergenerational experience provided by the exhibition and associated activities thus provided a venue for media awareness and the need to be critical viewers, as opposed to passive and inarticulate consumers.

Gilbert's Travels: Approaching the Artist's Story

The 2003 Tweed retrospective exhibition, *Gilbert Munger: Quest for Distinction,* curated by Peter Spooner, was an interdisciplinary adventure that integrated 19th century American landscape painting with geology, geography, and American history. Buried in Duluth, Gilbert Munger was one of the first American artists to paint the West: he was commissioned to accompany Clarence King when King conducted the United States Geological Survey of the Fortieth Parallel in 1869-1870. Munger also painted with Albert Bierstadt at the Donner Pass. His painting was widely celebrated in both Europe and America, where he won numerous medals and awards before dying—and he died, surprisingly, forgotten by the world of art. The Tweed exhibition was the first retrospective exhibition of his work ever given.

During the fall semester of 2003, all art education classes focused attention on the Munger exhibition. There were gallery talks by curators, art historians, and geologists. In addition to their own gallery drawings and landscape painting assignments, the students were required to create interdisciplinary lessons based on the exhibition. They studied maps, geological land formations, the Westward Expansion, and 19th Century landscape painting techniques. Students also assisted with the free Munger family day program at the museum. During this event, students assisted children with activities at the learning stations. Together, they built toothpaste volcanoes and a clay replica of a mountain range; they also took part in a Munger treasure hunt, explored State floor puzzles of America, created their own Western landscapes, and made Munger medals.

As featured guests, two art education students dressed up as Gilbert Munger (see Figure 12.5). One student dramatized the younger Munger as he looked in America and the other dramatized the older Munger in Europe. These two students gave theatrical living history tours in character, telling the story of

Munger's travels around the world and discussing his painting technique in relation to specific paintings. In creating these theatrical tours, they imaginatively brought Munger back to life exactly 100 years after his death (Spooner, 2003).

Figure: 12.5. Gilbert Munger (Chris Detert and Lucas Anderson)

Conclusion: Looking Behind the Tomato Curtain to See and Make Art

By invigorating art education methods courses with these kinds of museum-based, inclusive learning experiences, we made significant steps towards realizing the goal of strengthening community connections through interdisciplinary and intergenerational learning activities. We have also begun to develop an alternative model for teacher training and intergenerational learning. This new model differs from the traditional art teacher-student relationship to one that promotes reciprocal learning for both age groups through the direct contact with original, and inclusive, works of art.

Because our education program involving the Tweed Museum is committed to offering diverse "opportunities for experiential learning and interactive inquiry"

(Jeffers, 2003, p. 19), it is able to foster and develop what Elliot Eisner called "genuinely creative approaches to education" (Eisner & Hobbs, 1986, p. 49). The art museum, as Eisner put it, can "contribute in many and diverse ways to the well being of the community. The museum helps reshape society" (p. 44). We have used the Tweed Museum for just this purpose. As a university art museum, it has a unique potential for helping to develop visually-sensitive and culturally-engaged future teachers who, we hope, will continue to "look behind the tomato curtain" to enrich their curriculum with imagination and creativity.

References

Berry, N., & Mayer, S. (1989). *Museum education history, theory, and practice.* Reston, VA: National Art Education Association.

Boyd-Brent, J., & Shen, L. (2001). *Here by Design.* The Goldstein Museum of Design. Minneapolis, MN: Department of Design, Housing, and Apparel. University of Minnesota.

Burton, J. M. (2000). The configuration of meaning: Learner-centered art education revisited. *Studies in Art Education, 41*(4), 330-345.

Delacruz, E. M. (1997). Design for inquiry: Instructional theory, research and practice in art education. Reston, VA: National Art Education Association.

Eisner, E. W., & Dobbs, S. M. (1986). Museum education in twenty American art Museums. *Museum News, 65*(2), 42-49.

Gude, O. (2004). Postmodern principles: In search of a 21st century art education. *Art Education, 57*(1), 6-13.

Jeffers, C. (2003). Gallery as nexus. *Art Education, 56*(1), 19-24.

Gaudelius Y., & Speirs, P. (Eds.). (2002). *Contemporary issues in art.* Upper Saddle River, NJ: Prentice Hall.

Sipe, L. (2001). Using picture books to teach art history. *Studies in Art Education, 42*(3), 197-209.

Spooner, P. F. (2004). *Fifty Years/Fifty Artworks: Tweed Museum of Art Collection.* Duluth, MN: Tweed Museum of Art, University of Minnesota Duluth.

Spooner, P. F. (2003). *Munger Exhibition* [brochure]. Duluth, MN: Tweed Museum of Art, University of Minnesota Duluth.

Waterfall, M., & Grusin, S. (1991). *Where's the me in museum: Going to the museum with children.* Arlington, VA: Vandamere Press.